Seeing Writing

Seeing Writing

LEWIS MEYERS

Hunter College

 HARCOURT BRACE JOVANOVICH, INC.

New York   San Diego   Chicago   San Francisco   Atlanta
London   Sydney   Toronto

To Diana

PREFACE

Seeing Writing offers a new and simple approach to the common problems of basic composition. As the title suggests, the book uses visual methods—specifically, uncaptioned cartoon drawings—as an organizing principle. The drawings themselves are as varied as the skills they teach. They range from a Rube Goldberg diagram in Writing Project One that requires students to use particular sentence forms in describing a process, to a drawing by William Steig in Writing Project Six that calls for comparison and contrast and uses of the active and passive voice. Unlike the use of visual materials in other textbooks, the drawings in *Seeing Writing* create complete and carefully organized writing projects for students. Several lessons in grammar and composition are taught in each writing project by one drawing; and in each writing project a series of instructional steps carefully leads students from prewriting to the actual editing of their essays.

The drawings are intended to provide the discipline of highly structured composition. But they also allow room for the students' own creativity. In practice, students match ideas and concepts with the meaning implied in the drawings. Consequently, they learn to think originally instead of merely duplicating the ideas of others, which is often the case when prose models are used exclusively to stimulate writing. For instance, the essential conflict between an optimist and a pessimist may be understood from one drawing and how people often meet the past in the present from another. These concepts are not unfamiliar to students; yet by actually forming and organizing these concepts in an essay, they learn how to write coherently about them.

Drawings are generally more accessible than essays to those college students who are inadequately prepared in reading. But even more important, drawings like those in *Seeing Writing* enable students to continue a single line of thought from beginning to end of an essay. A drawing with a man tied to a question mark, for example, suggests one kind of human predicament and marks out the path for students to follow in their discussion.

Drawings also help illustrate grammatical points and rhetorical modes. A man on the edge of a cliff teaches the difference between verb tenses. And when two people react differently to the same situation, the use of comparison and contrast is made evident. What is graphic is memorable. The drawings, therefore, have the practical advantage of aiding the retention as well as the acquisition of writing skills.

From Writing Project Six onward, the drawings are supplemented by texts and writing topics. These may be assigned when instructors judge students ready to write capably about them. The texts and topics, like the drawings, suggest a broader meaning and so also require conceptual thinking.

Seeing Writing is designed so that students may work individually or as a class. Students produce writing throughout a given writing project, not merely at its end, and composition is accomplished in a step-by-step fashion. This organization gives instructors the choice of establishing discussion or workshop formats, and of breaking the class into small groups and bringing it together again at any STEP. Each STEP directs students to complete a particular writing task. They may be asked to write a topic sentence with special attention to the selection of details; or, they may be required to express a concrete relationship in a drawing in conceptual terms. Some STEPs require students to check their writing for grammar and style. Other STEPs ask students to interpret meaning by answering questions about significant details and their relationships within a drawing, text, or writing topic. At the end of each Writing Project, a STEP asks students to edit, revise, and rewrite their essays. Whatever the STEP asks, and however long the instructor decides to spend on it, no STEP is taken until the previous one has been completed.

Although the text is sequential, each project is self-contained and may be used independently of the others. The earlier projects focus on basic grammar, conceptualization, and paragraph structure. Later projects emphasize the thesis sentence, the complete essay, and rhetorical modes. All the projects create the same situation for students who use this book: a total involvement in writing.

I would like to thank Clayton Hudnall of the University of Hartford for reading an earlier version of this book, and the staff at Harcourt Brace Jovanovich for their patience and expert help in preparing *Seeing Writing*. In particular, I am grateful to my editors, Drake Bush and Bob Beitcher; to my copy editors, Lee Shenkman and Jenny Peters-Jenks; to the art and design staff, Pat Smythe, Richard Lewis, and Dorothea von Elbe; and to the production manager, Nancy Edmunds Kalal.

L. M.

CONTENTS

WRITING PROJECT ONE	# Sentence Forms; Sentence Variety; Describing a Process

Write a paragraph describing the process shown by the following diagram. (An alternative drawing may be found on p. 16). Use different sentence forms in the composition.

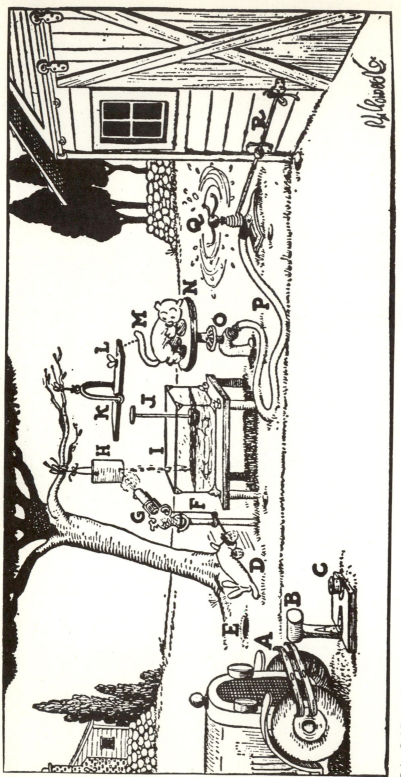

Rube Goldberg

Rube Goldberg is responsible for this diagram, but the person who planned what happens in it is Goldberg's fictional creation from the 1920s, Professor Lucifer Butts. Evidently, Professor Butts thought that the scheme depicted by the diagram was sensible. We may disagree with him, and probably we expect other people to think as we do about the diagram. But no one will be able to express one opinion or another unless we can describe what is going on in the diagram. This is what we always do first with schemes, plans, systems, and projects: we describe what they are like.

Nouns and Verbs

If we look at the diagram for a few moments, we will notice it has several important features. First, there are various objects within the frame. Second, each object is separated from the other, and yet we can imagine each object acting upon the next one. And finally, we observe that at the end of this string of connections a definite event will occur.

To name the objects in this diagram is to use *nouns*:

> bumper
>
> cap   (The text originally accompanying the diagram explains that the mallet (B) hits an exploding cap (C).)

To specify how these objects act upon each other is to use *verbs*:

> moves
>
> explodes

The nouns are now the subjects of these verbs. To put nouns as subjects together with verbs is to form *sentences*:

> The bumper moves.
>
> The cap explodes.

A sentence following the above examples will take us further into the diagram. The next sentence will take us further than that, and so on. By the end of a sequence of sentences, we will have accomplished in words what the diagram does in pictures: the description of a process.

> **STEP 1**   **Starting with the noun** *bumper*, **make a list of all the objects in the diagram. Opposite each object list the verb (start with** *move***) that describes what the object does. You may come up with more than one verb for each noun you list.**

The Sentence (1)

Before using our list of nouns and verbs to build sentences, we should examine the basic structure of the sentence itself. We recognize a sentence by the capital letter that begins it and the period, question mark, or exclamation point that ends it. A sentence, in other words, has definite boundaries. Every time we string words together within these boundaries, we are representing what we have written as a complete sentence. To see what is complete within boundaries, we can look at the simplest sentence form—*the basic sentence*. All other sentence forms are built on the basic sentence.

The Basic Sentence

The basic sentence is complete if it contains two main parts— *subject* and *verb*. In the sentence *The bumper moves*, the noun *bumper*, as we have seen, is the immediate subject of the verb *moves*.

Most of the time, however, both subject and verb have other words around them:

> The car bumper moves ahead to push down a mallet.

In this sentence, the word *car*, coming before *bumper*, fully describes the kind of bumper. It is used as an *adjective*—a word that describes or limits a noun or a pronoun. The word *ahead*, coming after the verb *moves*, provides us with a better sense of direction. *Ahead* is an *adverb*—a word that describes or limits a verb, an adjective, another adverb, or even an entire sentence. (Other examples of adverbs are *very, soon, too, always*, and most words ending in *-ly*.) Both *car* and *ahead*, and the rest of the sentence, *to* *push down a mallet*, give us a better understanding of what happens in the diagram than just *The bumper moves* would have.

In the previous example of the basic sentence, the verb *moves* does what the verb of any sentence has to do:

1. The verb identifies the subject of the sentence once we ask who or what is doing what the verb says is happening.
2. The verb shows the time—now, earlier, or later—in which the subject is acting.

STEP 2   Using the nouns and their matching verbs from your list, compose one basic sentence for each step in the process. You can start, if you wish, with *The car bumper moves ahead to push down a mallet*. After this, keep the time shown by your verbs consistent. When you finish, divide each sentence into subject part and verb part and tie the verb to the subject with an arrow:

The car bumper / moves ahead to push down a mallet.

The basic sentences composed in STEP 2 should have covered all the steps necessary to describe the action in the diagram and produce the final event. That is, even without consciously directing ourselves to do so, we have gone some distance toward describing the process. Before going on, we can pause to look at process itself as a form of description.

Process (1)

Process refers to the way in which events occur. A description of a process answers the question *how*? about a final event: how did it happen, or how does it work? One major characteristic of any process is that it is composed of different steps (as each project in this book is a process made up of different steps). Both in pictures and in written language, an account of each step is necessary if our readers are to understand fully. If one step is omitted or even poorly represented, then—for our audience—the string of connections snaps apart. In Rube Goldberg's diagram, for instance, omitting what happens to the water in the fish tank would prevent our audience from knowing how the process works itself out.

STEP 3   Go back to your basic sentences and check the steps those sentences represent to make sure that nothing is left out.

Keep the diagram in view as you do this. The capital letters in the diagram should have guided you forward, but one way to see if you progressed correctly is by starting at the end. From *R*, return first to *Q*, then to *P*, and so on, going back to the beginning as if you were running a film backward. Professional proofreaders often work in just this way.

The Sentence (2)

The Compound Sentence

The car bumper moves ahead to push down a mallet is the sentence that begins the description of this process. It has a subject and a verb that shows time. But it is not the only kind of sentence we can form. We know this ourselves if, having carefully observed what Rube Goldberg makes happen, we have wanted to connect the mallet going down with the cap going off. These two events are very close together in time and in space. Also, one event causes the other to happen. These facts can urge us to put the steps together in a single sentence. One way to do so is by doubling the basic sentence:

> The car bumper moves ahead to push down a mallet, and a cap explodes.

This doubling produces a *compound sentence*. A compound itself means two or more of the same element:

two or more nouns:

> mallet and cap

two or more verbs:

> explodes and scares

two or more adjectives:

> heavy and thick

or two or more basic sentences, as in the previous example.

When we join two basic sentences, each becomes a *clause*. Every clause must have both a subject and a verb. In the example sentence, one clause is *The car bumper moves ahead to push down a mallet*; the other clause is *a cap explodes*. These clauses are joined by a comma and the word *and*.

Besides *and*, there are a few other short linking words (traditionally called *coordinating conjunctions*) used with a comma to join clauses. These words are *but, for, so, or,* and *nor*:

> The mallet is aimed at a cap, so an explosion occurs.

Each of these coordinating conjunctions is three letters or less. This is a helpful reminder when we are punctuating the compound sentence and need to know when to use a comma.

The comma is essential punctuation in some compound sentences. In the sentence *The car bumper moves ahead to push down a mallet, and a cap explodes*, the comma warns our readers against thinking that the bumper pushes down *both* a mallet and a cap; it also indicates that *and* joins two clauses, not two nouns.

And the comma, as we see again in the following example, always comes in front of the coordinating conjunction:

> The cap explodes with a bang, for the mallet strikes it directly.

Another method of joining clauses is by using longer linking words (traditionally called *adverbial conjunctions*) and transitional phrases. Some of these longer linking words are *afterwards, also, besides, consequently, furthermore, however, indeed, moreover, nevertheless, otherwise, still, subsequently, then, therefore,* and *thus*:

> The car bumper moves ahead to push down a mallet; then, a cap explodes.

> The mallet strikes the cap directly; consequently, the cap explodes with a bang.

Some of the transitional phrases are *in addition, in fact, on the other hand, on the contrary, as a result,* and *for example*:

> The car bumper moves ahead to push down a mallet; as a result, a cap explodes.

> The car bumper hits a mallet; in fact, the bumper pushes the mallet down.

As we see in the above examples, each of these longer linking words and transitional phrases is preceded by a semicolon (;) and followed by a comma (,).

The semicolon makes a stronger break than a comma does. This break tells our readers whether to read the linking word or transitional phrase as part of the first clause or as part of the second one. This is an important distinction to make. For instance, we do not want our readers to think the car bumper moving ahead is the second step:

> The car bumper moves ahead to push down a mallet then; a cap explodes.

And we do not want our readers to believe the movement of the car is *opposed* to something that happened before it:

> The car bumper hits a mallet, however; the mallet does not break.

Both *then* and *however* belong to the *second* clause.

A comma is used *after* the linking word or transitional phrase to separate them from the second clause, which has its own business to take care of. As a reminder, we should notice that each clause in this sentence has a subject and a verb.

It should be kept in mind that linking words and transitional phrases can be used in other ways in sentences. That is, they do not always link clauses to form compound sentences. Sometimes they begin sentences:

> As a result, the mallet is pushed down.

Other times, they come in the middle of sentences:

> The cap, therefore, explodes.

And sometimes they come at the end:

> Everything else in the process happens afterwards.

Care must be taken, therefore, to use a semicolon before longer linking words or transitional phrases *only* when there is a clause on either side of it.

A final method for forming a compound sentence is to use the semicolon by itself between clauses:

> Rube Goldberg drew this diagram; the professor planned the action in it.

All punctuation marks are signals to the reader. Most commonly, the semicolon coming between two groups of words signals that these groups are both clauses with a subject and a verb. Using the semicolon is a good idea when we want to emphasize the close relation of points, such as the connection between the movement of the bumper and the explosion of the cap, or the connection between the responsibility of the artist and the character.

The semicolon used alone, without linking word or transitional phrase, is also effective when attempting wit:

> Professor Butts saw connections; we make them.

And always, the semicolon used alone produces the impact of pistonlike statements.

On the other hand, a comma used alone between groups of words most often indicates that one of the groups is *not* a clause, as we see in the following sentence:

> Many years ago, Rube Goldberg drew this diagram.

Many years ago is not a clause; therefore, it can be followed by a comma.

To sum up, the three methods of dividing the two or more clauses into a compound sentence are:

1. comma and coordinating conjunction:

   > The car bumper moves ahead to push down a mallet, and a cap explodes.

2. semicolon, long linking word (adverbial conjunction) or transitional phrase, and comma:

   > The cap has to explode; otherwise, nothing else would happen.

   > The noise cannot be low; on the contrary, it must be loud enough to scare the rabbit.

3. semicolon used alone:

   > Everything else does happen; nothing is left out.

The compound sentence is one in which clauses are balanced like a see-saw, with the person on one end weighing the same as the person on the other. Such a balance indicates that the point one clause makes is no more and no less important than the point made by the other clause. In writing a composition, we use compound sentences when this balance and this equal importance are what we see as the reality of the subject matter.

STEP 4   Write one compound sentence for each pair of basic sentences you composed in STEPS 2 and 3. Your first compound sentence should closely resemble *The car bumper moves ahead to push down a mallet; a cap explodes.* Employ all three methods of writing compound sentences discussed above.

Some words joining clauses that you may find particularly use-ful are *and, thus, therefore, consequently, then, as a result*. There are, of course, other words and transitional phrases that you might employ.

Process (2)

The first necessary part of describing a process is listing the series of steps. The second part is specifying the relationships be-tween these steps. In STEP 4, the compound sentences estab-lished relationships, showing how in any process each step de-pends on the one before it. For instance, *then* reveals that one event happened *after* another (time); *as a result*, reveals that one event happens *because* of another (cause and effect); *and* shows that one event is simply *added* to another (addition). Unless we make such relationships clear, our readers will be left with the impression that the various steps occur further apart in time and space than they really do, or that there is no necessary causal link between them. Since much of the thinking and writing we do is concerned with how one event or idea leads to another, we can imagine how im-portant it is to be able to show these relationships.

> **STEP 5**   Return to the compound sentences you just composed and note the different relationships you used in each. Could you have shown a different relationship? How could you have done so?

Often enough, the compound sentence does not make the exact kind of link between steps we want, and we need a different sen-tence form: the complex sentence.

The Sentence (3)

The Complex Sentence

Like the compound sentence, the complex sentence also con-sists of two or more clauses. Only, as the following sentence shows, there is a difference:

> The action starts when the cap explodes.

The first, or main clause, is *The action starts*; the second clause is *when the cap explodes*. Because the second clause begins with *when*, a *subordinating conjunction*, it turns the set it begins into a *subordinate clause*. *When* enables the subordinate clause to say something *about* the other clause. In the above example, *when the cap explodes* tells the time the action starts: *when* is the word that relates the subordinate clause to the main clause.

Unlike the compound sentence, the clauses in a complex sentence are not equal. It is as if the subordinating conjunction pulled the clause it begins down from the main clause:

The action starts *when the cap explodes.*

Because the subordinate clause depends on the main clause, it cannot be written alone as a sentence.

Some of the more common subordinating conjunctions are *after, although, as, as if, because, before, even if, even though, if, now that, once, since, so that, that, though, unless, until, when, where, which, while, who*. As is clear from this list, some subordinating conjunctions are two words rather than one.

We can better understand how the complex sentence is formed if we turn back to the pair of basic sentences and the compound sentence we made from them:

> BASIC The car bumper moves ahead to push down a mallet.
> A cap explodes.

> COMPOUND The car bumper moves ahead to push down a mallet;
> a cap explodes.

The complex sentence adds a subordinating conjunction at the *beginning* of one of the clauses and removes the semicolon and/or linking word from between the two clauses:

> COMPLEX After the car bumper moves ahead to push down a
> mallet, a cap explodes.

The word *after* tells our readers that the action of the cap follows the action of the bumper. We also might have written:

> Because the car bumper moves ahead to push down a mallet,
> a cap explodes.

Because tells us that the action of the bumper is the *cause* of the cap exploding.

STEP 6   Return to the second compound sentence you wrote. For practice, turn it into a complex sentence.

As mentioned above, each subordinating conjunction shows how the clause it begins relates to the main clause. It is best to discover these relationships through use, but we must be careful about which clause we subordinate. For instance, if we wrote *The car bumper moves ahead to push down a mallet because a cap explodes*, we would be reversing the actual cause-and-effect relationship. We would be reversing the order of events if we wrote *The car bumper moves ahead to push down a mallet after a cap explodes*.

There are three positions within a complex sentence for the subordinate clause: the beginning, the end, and in the middle:

> BEGINNING   Once the car bumper moves ahead to push down a mallet, a cap explodes.
>
> END   A cap explodes after a car bumper moves ahead to push down a mallet.
>
> MIDDLE   A cap, after the car bumper moves ahead to push down a mallet, explodes.

The end of a sentence is usually where we place whatever point we want to emphasize. Depending on emphasis, then, we choose one position rather than another for a subordinate clause in a complex sentence.

In the first example, a comma separates the subordinate clause from the main clause. The comma is often used in this position to avoid any possible confusion we might have about where one clause ends and the next clause begins. For instance, the following sentence is clear because the comma causes our readers to pause after the word *this*:

> Although Rube Goldberg drew this, Professor Butts planned it.

But the lack of a comma might lead our readers to include Professor Butts within the subordinate clause:

> Although Rube Goldberg drew this Professor Butts

The possibility of confusion is not usually great when the subordinate clause ends the sentence, and so most of the time the comma is not needed between the main clause and the subordinate clause. And as we see in the third example, commas *surround* a subordinate clause that comes in the middle of the sentence.

STEP 7 **Starting with the two complex sentences already examined, turn each of your compound sentences from STEP 4 into a complex sentence. Some subordinating conjunctions you might find particularly useful are** *after, because, since, while, once, so that,* **and** *when.* **Be sure to punctuate your new sentences correctly. Keep the diagram in view while you perform this step so that you can be absolutely clear about the relationship between clauses in each sentence.**

Sentence Variety

We now have used three different sentence forms to describe the same process. The next move is to mix these forms to produce a single description. For although there are many ways to write, including using the same sentence form several times in a row, most good writing has variety. Sentence variety helps to maintain the interest of the audience; too much repetition is boring. Variety also meets the needs of subject matter when the difference between making one point and making the next can be shown by the way we join clauses. For instance, a compound sentence would work well to describe the first two steps:

> A car bumper moves ahead to push down a mallet, and a cap explodes.

But a complex sentence describing the first two steps might confuse our readers about their importance:

> Once a car bumper moves ahead to push down a mallet, a cap explodes.

Here, *once* subordinates the action of the car bumper and leaves our readers with the false impression that the step responsible for starting the whole process is less important than the one that comes after it. On the other hand, writing a compound sentence to describe these two steps puts equal emphasis on each step.

To describe the very last event in the diagram, a basic sentence might be very effective. It would carry a note of finality that seems appropriate to the last step in any process.

As we write a description of the diagram using different sentence forms, we can ask ourselves the following questions:

1. Have we identified what we are describing as a diagram and said who the artist is? Probably we could do this in the first sentence, before we begin to describe the process.

2. Would our readers be certain about the location of all the objects in the diagram? For instance, have we said the cap is *under* the mallet and the water container is hanging *over* the fish tank?
3. Have we used some imagination in our description? Though we want to record the steps and their relationships accurately, it is possible to make educated guesses about the size, speed, and force of various objects in the diagram.

We should be able to answer *yes* to all three questions. They suggest what we can do whenever we write. Later in these writing projects, the introductions will be longer, relations shown throughout a composition may be abstract instead of concrete, and imagination may have more with which to work. If we practice within the limits available now, we should be able to write more ambitiously later.

STEP 8   Compose the final version of this description of Rube Goldberg's diagram by combining different sentence forms. Go back to your preliminary drafts of basic, compound, and complex sentences (a *draft* is one stage along the way of a finished composition), and work from them. Make sure again of the relationships between steps that you are showing. Check your knowledge by looking at the diagram as you write.

Interproject | *Fragments and Run-On Sentences*

The following drawing is an alternative for Writing Project One.

Drawing by Handelsman; © 1978 The New Yorker Magazine, Inc.

In writing basic, compound, and complex sentences, there are two kinds of serious errors: one is the *sentence fragment*; the other is the *run-on sentence*.

Sentence Fragments

Sentence fragments leave our readers without enough information to go on. One kind of sentence fragment is a sentence lacking a subject and/or a verb that shows definite time. The following are examples of sentence fragments:

> Pushes down a mallet.

The subject of the verb *pushes* is missing. The sentence should read: *The car bumper pushes down a mallet*.

> The car bumper pushing down a mallet.

The verb *pushing* does not show a definite time. It is a *present participle*. Verbs ending with *-ing* need to be changed to another form of the verb (*pushes, pushed,* or *will push*). Or the present participle needs a helping verb in front of it (*is pushing, was pushing, will be pushing* are some examples). The change we make shows whether the time is now, earlier, or later. The various verb tenses are discussed in Writing Project Five.

Another kind of fragment is a sentence consisting of *only* a subordinate clause:

> Because the car bumper pushes down a mallet.

There are both a subject and a verb in the above sentence, but the word *because* subordinates the clause. There must be another clause in the sentence, one *not* beginning with a subordinating conjunction, if the sentence is to be complete. The sentence should read: *Because the car bumper pushes down a mallet, the cap explodes*.

A third kind of fragment is a compound sentence without a verb showing definite time in one of the clauses:

> The car bumper pushes down a mallet, and the cap exploding.

Here the first clause is correct, but the second one has only a present participle. That clause should read: *and the cap explodes*.

EXERCISE

1. Correct the sentence fragments that follow. When necessary, add a clause to complete the sentence:

- **a.** This diagram showing one action after another.
- **b.** Once we look closely at each object.
- **c.** The objects old-fashioned.
- **d.** Goes from one step to the next in a fairly complicated way.
- **e.** This process alphabetically from capital letter to capital letter.
- **f.** Appearing originally in a magazine.
- **g.** That magazine no longer in circulation.
- **h.** The animal looking like a rabbit.
- **i.** Because the water rises.
- **j.** The process has come a long way, and this the end result.

Run-On Sentences

A run-on sentence is a compound sentence that lacks the correct punctuation and/or linking words between the two clauses. Most often, a run-on sentence confuses the relationship between the two clauses. The following sentences are run-on's:

> The car bumper pushes down a mallet, the cap explodes.

A comma cannot separate two clauses unless it is followed by a coordinating conjunction (*and* or *but*, for example).

> The car bumper pushes down a mallet the cap explodes.

Without some conjunction or punctuation mark between *mallet* and *the*, our readers could not know what concludes the first step in the process. A semicolon (;) alone would work in this position.

> The car bumper pushes down a mallet right away the cap explodes.

Here, our readers would not know whether *right away* belongs with the first clause (and therefore with the first step) or with the second clause (and step). A semicolon in front of *right* and a comma after *away* are necessary.

EXERCISES

2. Write a corrected version of the following run-on sentences.

  a. This diagram shows one action after another, they all are interlocked.
  b. We should look at each object carefully, then we can imagine what each object does.
  c. The objects in this diagram are clearly drawn it is easy therefore to recognize each.
  d. We go from one action to the next in a fairly complicated way this process moves on to conclude simply.
  e. The car has an old-fashioned radiator, that is the grill is not at all streamlined.
  f. Because the objects in the diagram are not usually found in the same place, the process stands out as a strange one in fact, it looks unreal.
  g. The original diagram was printed in Colliers that magazine was very popular and widely read it is no longer in existence.

3. The following passage describing a process contains many sentence fragments and run-on sentences. Rewrite the paragraph, correcting each error. Add linking words as well as punctuation when necessary.

> When I brush my dog. I start from the back on one side. I brush her tail first, then I brush a hind leg. At the bottom of the paw, I brush the fur back with my left hand. If when I do this I notice matted fur. I brush it out first. Then I work my way up her leg. Pushing the fur back and brushing it forward again in waves. From the hind leg, I move to her body, her stomach needs to be done first. Again, I work up from the bottom. I do her side. Until I reach the ridge of her back. I brush her foreleg the same way I did her hind leg. Her neck and ears come next. The ears are delicate, they have to be brushed very carefully. Last comes her head, and then I start all over. On the other side.

4. Extend the process depicted by Rube Goldberg in this diagram. Describe each additional step clearly and carefully. In this passage, use all three sentence forms studied in this project.

The Topic Sentence; Description; Pronouns

Write a paragraph describing the drawing on the following page. (An alternative drawing may be found on p. 35.) Use a topic sentence to begin the paragraph, and make accurate use of pronouns as part of the description.

Steven Guarnaccia

In the English language, *seeing* sometimes refers to mental understanding as well as to physical eyesight. When someone explains a point to us, for instance, we might answer with "I see what you mean." In writing, we can enable our readers to see what we mean only if we have first described what we want them to understand. Otherwise, they will be confused about our starting point. Description, then, precedes interpretation. It is the focus for this writing project.

Description (1)

In Writing Project One, describing a process, we knew where to start our composition and where to end it. We also knew what we had to include in our paragraph. With the drawing in this project, however, new problems arise. Which details should we put in as part of a description? Which should we leave out? What should we mention first? In what order should we describe the details? These are problems we face with every descriptive task.

Always, we must decide what our audience needs to know. When we describe a drawing, we should think of it as one only we can see. Then our readers must depend solely on our words to know what we know. With this in mind, the first decision to make is which details to include. Here that means which details of the drawing's physical appearance. The second decision is in what order to put these details.

Details

On any list of details we compile after looking at Steven Guarnaccia's drawing, we will certainly include the word *wagon*; and, the word *city* will no doubt be on our list as well. These are the most obvious details in the drawing. But they are not the only details. Within both the wagon and the city there are still smaller details: smaller but not less important. Just to state that there are different buildings, for instance, is to go into more detail about the city. Precision of this sort is always necessary. And here, we have to do more than simply mention the buildings. We have to say what *kind* of buildings they are. If we do not, we might lead our readers to assume that the city looks very different from the way it actually does.

> **STEP 1**   Observe the drawing carefully. List all its details. If any one detail can be broken down into even smaller details, expand your list by doing so. Take, for example, the aquarium from the diagram in Writing Project One: it can be broken down into two fish, water, floating cork, and plank table.

It is always necessary to avoid losing our readers' interest, but that is a real danger if the need to refer several times in a row to one object, event, idea, or person produces a boring repetitiveness. Luckily, every language offers different names—synonyms—for any one detail. English is no exception. Synonyms can keep up interest by presenting variety. Also, however, synonyms call attention to different ideas of what is named. For instance, of the several terms in use for the wagons in this picture, one of them, *prairie schooner*, gives an idea of the vehicles as sailing ships. Other details in the drawing also have various names.

> **STEP 2**   Try to come up with synonyms for details in the drawing. Make a list of the synonyms and, by looking them up in a dictionary, attempt to discover the different idea of the same detail each one offers. If you can, use these synonyms to vary the descriptive detail in your paragraph.

By now we may have collected many details or, perhaps, just a few. If many, then our list probably has met its most important challenge: *completeness*. Other tests the list must pass are *accuracy* and *specificity*.

Accuracy   Written details are accurate if they have a one-to-one relationship with the actual objects or events they describe. To say the sun rises, for instance, is not a strictly accurate way of describing the factual relationship between a stationary star and a revolving planet. Though no one will criticize us for referring to the dawn in this way, we would be criticized—and rightly so—if we said the animals in the present drawing were cattle.

Specificity   Written details can be general and vague, or they can closely identify what they describe. The door in the Rube Goldberg diagram, for instance, acquires a specific character when we say it is a *garage door*. If we mention the kind of buildings in Steven Guarnaccia's drawing, we will be more specific in the present paragraph.

STEP 3 **Check your details for completeness, accuracy, and specificity. Match your list against the drawing itself. If you find that you have not been specific enough about any one detail, you might want to add further details. Make any other changes you think necessary.**

Our list should now be in good order. But it might not be in the right order. The eye skips from one object to the next and then back to the first object; the mind repeats that movement; and the hand that writes obeys the mind. This happens naturally, and we understand what we are saying. But our readers—who want to read swiftly and without breaks—might not understand. As writers, we have to make conscious decisions for the sake of our readers. Therefore, at this point in gathering details, we begin to put them where they should be.

It may be, for instance, that our list starts with details of the wagons, proceeds to details of the city, and then returns to the wagons. If so, it is necessary to *group* details according to where they belong: all wagon details under the category *wagons*, and all city details under the category *city*. To use an example from Writing Project One, if we had been describing the objects in the diagram instead of showing their connections, our list would be confusing if we went from *two fish* to *plank table* to *rabbit* to *garage door* to *cork float*. The details of the aquarium would have to be collected under the title of that word itself. Grouping is a procedure that will become more difficult as the details we put together grow more abstract in nature. The details in Steven Guarnaccia's drawing, since they are concrete and therefore easier to group than ideas, give us good training for later tasks.

STEP 4 Do any details on your list require grouping? If so, group them now.

In addition to completeness, accuracy, and specificity as different ways to judge the quality of descriptive detail, there is one other way—*proper selection*. We meet this term now because to make a proper selection of details we must first have written a topic sentence to guide that selection.

The Topic Sentence

Most of us have heard of the topic sentence, and many of us have learned that its function is to state the main idea of a paragraph. We may have learned also that the other sentences in the paragraph support, develop, and illustrate that idea and none other. But admittedly this is all pretty vague, and if writing topic sentences has been a problem in the past it may be necessary to be more exact now about what they contain. Instead of worrying about what a "main idea" is, we should try to discover what is *in* the topic sentence that sentences following it are supposed to stick to.

Perhaps the best approach to the topic sentence is to describe it in the same way we would describe a chair, saying what it is made of (wood, metal, plastic) and what it is used for (sitting, standing on).

First, the topic sentence is indeed a sentence, with a subject and a verb. It is not a title.

Second, the topic sentence has two major parts—*topic* and *characterization*.

Third, the way these two parts act upon each other determines the use of the topic sentence.

We can see all of this in a topic sentence that could have been written for our paragraph in Writing Project One:

> The diagram by Rube Goldberg shows a series of mechanical steps that finally causes a garage door to open.

The *topic* is *The diagram by Rube Goldberg*. It is the subject matter of the paragraph and here identifies the artist—Rube Goldberg—and the form of his art—the diagram.

The *characterization* is *shows a series of mechanical steps that finally causes a garage door to open*. It is what we choose to say about the topic and states one important way of looking at it. We perform this function all the time in both speech and writing. We say, for instance, *She is tall*, or *The car is expensive*, or *He is a good teacher*. In each case, we are characterizing the person or object. In a topic sentence, this characteristic (*trait* or *feature* are synonyms) should be broad enough to deserve a whole paragraph. In the example of a topic sentence for Rube Goldberg's diagram, the characterization is of the picture's entire physical appearance. Other characterizations would have worked, including the feasibility of Professor Butts' scheme (*. . . shows the kind of plan that always will fail unless every single part of it works perfectly*) and the kind of person the professor himself was (*. . . shows an unusual mind at work*). These would interpret the practical and psychological meaning of the diagram. In this project, we are concerned with description, not interpretation, and so we should limit the characterization to appearance.

> **STEP 5** **Write the first draft of a topic sentence for this project's drawing. Identify the drawing and the artist in the topic part of your sentence. Characterize the drawing by its physical appearance. Since the wagons and the city have an important connection, try to describe it in the characterization. Make sure the sentence you have written is complete.**

We now can make a proper selection of details for this paragraph.

Every selection of details is based on the second part of the topic sentence—the characterization. Two points we must remember are these:

1. Whatever we put into the characterization has to be discussed somewhere in the paragraph.
2. Whatever we leave out of the characterization should *not* be discussed in the paragraph.

The characterization *shows a series of mechanical steps that finally causes a garage door to open* promises that we will cover all the steps and show their end result. If we had written only *shows a series of mechanical steps*, then we might find ourselves not mentioning the end of the process—opening a garage door—at all. We have two needs, therefore:

1. To make the characterization as complete as possible.
2. To make the statement in the characterization a general one.

If we were writing a topic sentence about Mr. X's table manners, we probably would not say in the characterization that Mr. X eats broccoli with his fingers. We would not, that is, if we wanted the characterization to include the whole of Mr. X's eating habits. Rather, we would try to be more general and write something like *Mr. X eats like a barbarian in a comic strip*. Mentioning that Mr. X uses his fingers gives only one detail of his eating habits, one that should not lead off the paragraph but be part of it.

For a proper selection of details in a paragraph for this writing project, the topic sentence should mention the chief details in the drawing. If they are mentioned, then we can write about them.

STEP 6 **Take another look at your topic sentence for this paragraph. Make sure the characterization of the drawing's appearance is general enough and that it contains everything you need to discuss in more detail as you write your paragraph. After you check this, return to your list and cross out any detail that does not *support*, *develop*, and *illustrate* what is in the characterization. For instance, if you had included in your list that the frame was a certain width and a certain length, that particular fact would be out of place in the body of the paragraph. So would any mention of what the drawing *means*, since the characterization for this paragraph involves physical appearance only.**

Having selected details based on the characterization (of course, there may have been no need to cross out any detail), it should now be clear that completeness of detail is less important than proper selection, since sometimes we must sacrifice the first to the second.

One final point to make regards the precision of language used in the characterization. Take, for instance, the word *mechanical* in the characterization of the topic sentence for Rube Goldberg's diagram (*shows a series of mechanical steps that finally causes a garage door to open*). *Mechanical* precisely indicates the kind of process; it helps distinguish the process from others that might have the same purpose but that go about it in a different way. With this point and the others we have made in mind, we can take a last look at our topic sentence and at our list of details as those details relate to the characterization.

STEP 7 In your topic sentence, use a precise word to depict the link between the two main parts of the drawing. Be careful to use the right word. For instance, though "speeding" is more precise than "going," "speeding" would not be exact for your purpose here. What word would be exact? Also, review your list of details again and see if there is any detail on it that is really too specific, too "small," to use in the characterization of your topic sentence. If you have used such a detail, restore it to your list for use in the body of the paragraph.

Description (2)

Order

We are now ready to decide on the order in which we will present the details of the drawing. The specific question we have to answer for our descriptive purpose is: do we mention the city or the wagons first? Our decision should respond to the needs of our readers and also to those of the subject matter. Let us see what those needs mean here.

In Writing Project One, chronology (time order) and causality (cause and effect) helped to decide the order we followed in describing the process in the diagram. The steps in that process went alphabetically from one capital letter to another (spatial order). But for the "wagon" drawing, time doesn't seem to be an issue in *describing* the picture; and nothing *causes* anything else to happen. There is, however, still a spatial relationship between the city and the wagons. If this relationship is revealed in the topic sentence, then the order for the details of the paragraph is defined, an order that responds to the needs of the subject matter.

There should not be any contradiction between those needs and the needs of our readers. But if there ever is, probably our readers should come first. Two major needs of the audience are:

1. To be able to follow our line of thought without having to double back or look ahead for further explanation.
2. To be able to move from sentence to sentence with *increasing* interest. If interest fails to increase, it does not stay the same but declines. And then the value of what has been written is lost.

In our paragraph, we will make reading easier if the order of details is consistent, that is, if we say everything about one object in the drawing first, and then everything about another object. But if our paragraph goes from city to wagons and then back to city, our readers will lose track of the wagons when they have to return to the city. This aspect of ordering ought not to be too difficult for us if beforehand we have grouped details correctly.

To keep up interest, and even to increase it, we should start from the least important detail and lead up to the most important or startling detail. For instance, if we are describing a person who has a dramatic hairdo but who otherwise is quite ordinary, it might be a good idea to start at the feet and work upwards. In the drawing for this project, we have to decide which detail—wagons or city—is the most important or startling.

> **STEP 8**   Put in order the details you have previously observed and grouped. For later use, write down next to them, or on another piece of paper, the following *prepositions* that describe spatial relationships. Note which of your details these words fit: *(in the) background/foreground, next to, besides, under, underneath, across from, above, in front of, behind, near.* These words can be used at the beginning of sentences, to connect with sentences coming before them.

At this point, before going on to write a paragraph describing the "wagon" drawing, we should pause to consider a part of speech that we probably had little occasion to use in Writing Project One, but which will no doubt prove necessary to writing now. That part of speech is the *pronoun*.

Pronouns

In Writing Project One, the forward movement of the process made it unnecessary for the most part to refer to an object we had already named. If we had been forced to look back very often, doubtless we would have been using pronouns. Writing Project Two, despite the fact that it depicts movement, describes a static drawing. The wagons and the city each have an individual existence and a spatial relationship that requires a more lengthy inspection. And when we do go into something more deeply we often refer to it, or to parts of it, in the same sentence or in the following one. In doing so, we use pronouns.

In the paragraph for this project, for instance, we might write a sentence like the following:

> This is the big city.

If we then want to say something about the city, our next sentence could include either the same words, *the big city*, or one word, *it*. *It* is the better choice since it avoids needless repetition of words already used.

> The big city can be frightening to newcomers.

> It can also be frightening to longtime residents.

Here is a chart of personal pronouns. No doubt every word in it is familiar. Though we use all of these pronouns every day, in writing as well as in speaking, we may not always use them effectively and accurately. If this is true, we can always refer to this chart to check our usage.

Pronoun Chart

Number	SINGULAR			PLURAL		
Case	subjective	objective	possessive	subjective	objective	possessive
Person 1	I	me	my, mine	we	us	our, ours
2	you	you	your, yours	you	you	your, yours
3	he, she, it	him, her, it	his, her, hers its	they	them	their, theirs

STEP 9 Return to your list of details for the drawing in this project. Next to each detail, list the subjective, objective, and possessive pronouns that would refer to it.

> EXAMPLE The city   it, it, its

> The wagons   they, them, their

Look at the drawing while you complete this STEP. If necessary, also consult the pronoun chart.

Person, Number, and Case

PERSON   We use *person* in pronouns to point out the person or object to whom or to which we are referring. If we say, "I am speaking to you about him," *I* is the speaker and is in the first person; *you* is the person to whom we are speaking and is in the second person; and *he* is the person about whom we are speaking and is in the third person.

In this drawing, each detail is an *it* or a *they*. We should notice that the third person (see the chart) can refer to *things* as well as to people. No noun on our list of details can be referred to by a *you*.

Using *you* will sometimes confuse our readers if it is not them in particular but people in general to whom we want to refer. To be clear, we can substitute *one* (and then *he* or *she* to refer to *one*), *we, an individual, person, people,* or particular words like *viewer, reader,* or *listener.*

NUMBER   *Number* (in using pronouns) is a term that describes how *many* of anything we are referring to at one time. We use *they* to refer to *all* the wagons in the drawing because there are more than one of them. We use *it* to refer to *one* wagon at a time. Here is one example. If we were describing the capital letters in the diagram for Writing Project One, we might write:

> Capital letters guide the viewer through the diagram. They proceed alphabetically within it.

Plural *they* refers to *capital letters*; singular *it* stands for *diagram.*

STEP 10   **Return to your list of nouns and the pronouns that refer to them. Without consulting your chart this time, indicate every singular series of pronouns with an *S*, and every plural series with a *P*. After you do this, check them against the chart. Then match your nouns and pronouns with the objects in the drawing and check to see whether both nouns and pronouns show the correct number. For example:**

> The city   it, it, its   S   **correct**

CASE   *Case* is the term that describes the kind of work that pronouns do in the sentence.

A pronoun in the *subjective* case (see Writing Project One, p. 3) acts as the subject of a verb:

> In the background, a city rises up. It looks like New York.

It, referring to *city*, is the subject of the verb *looks*.

A pronoun in the *objective* case follows a verb or a preposition:

> We all recognize it.

It is the object of the verb *recognize* because it answers the question *what*? We all recognize what? *It*.

> Some of us are all too aware of it.

Us and *it* are each the object of the preposition *of*.

A pronoun in the *possessive* case shows ownership:

> But this is our city, like it or not.

The above form of the pronoun (see the chart) comes into use when the thing owned comes *after* the pronoun.

> We should remember that this city is ours.

The second form of the pronoun—*ours*—is used when the thing owned comes *before* the pronoun.

Reflexive Pronouns

A *reflexive pronoun* refers to a noun or another pronoun that has already been mentioned. The reflexive pronouns are: *myself; yourself; himself, herself, itself; ourselves; yourselves; themselves*. For example:

> This city is a world in itself.

Itself refers to *city*. As in this case, reflexive pronouns are often used for additional emphasis.

As mentioned earlier, when writing in detail we use pronouns. Another way to put this is that pronouns *help* us to write more: they take us further on to develop both sentences and paragraphs. The next step in this project is for that purpose.

STEP 11   Write a sentence to follow your topic sentence. Then write a third sentence that uses at least one pronoun to refer to some detail you mentioned in the second sentence. For instance, if you said something about the city in the second sentence, you could conceivably use the possessive pronoun *its* in the sentence following it:

second sentence   The city looks like New York.
third sentence   Its buildings rise to the sky where they penetrate the clouds.

It is doubtful that you would write these particular sentences, but notice how *its* connects *buildings* to *city*, and how *they* connects the point about penetrating the clouds to the buildings and allows us to continue describing them both if we wish.

This brings us to the final step of this project.

STEP 12 **Starting with these completed sentences, write one paragraph describing the physical appearance of the drawing. As you write, refer to your list of details (which should include not only nouns but the pronouns that refer to them).**

The following Interproject contains information and practice exercises for checking topic sentence, pronoun use, and description. Turn to the Interproject once you finish this paragraph and check your usage. Following up on the first writing project, avoid run-on and fragmentary sentences, and try to use basic, compound, and complex sentences in your paragraph.

Interproject | *Using Pronouns*

The following drawing by Guy Billout is
an alternative for Writing Project Two.

Guy Billout

Guy Billout

EXERCISES

1. The following topic sentences were written for a paragraph describing the physical appearance of the drawing on the left.

  a. The drawing depicts a man on a bridge.
  b. Guy Billout's latest drawing shows a bridge, clouds, and several people.
  c. We see a man with his hands in his pockets meeting three other people on a causeway.
  d. The three people appear to be wearing crowns.
  e. This drawing by Guy Billout represents a strange occurrence.

For each of these topic sentences, ask yourself these questions, some of which require looking back to the drawing:

  a. Is the topic sentence a full sentence, with a subject and a verb?
  b. Is there a topic and a characterization for each sentence?
  c. Does the topic make as full an identification as possible?
  d. Does the characterization mention the most important objects in the picture?
  e. Does the characterization mention the relationship between the objects?

Locate the topic sentence that is most nearly correct. Rewrite it and adopt it, if you wish, as the topic sentence for a paragraph describing this drawing.

2. A list of details for the above paragraph would include the following:

bridge	hands in pockets
a man	long dress
three people	long shadow
clouds	shadows folding over bridge
arches	shadowed arches
causeway	railing
horizon line	a man in a shirt
one foot lifted	sky
black hair	sash
people in line	pants
Guy Billout	

a. Group the details in the above list according to categories you can establish for that purpose. For example:

category bridge

b. In what order would you put the details if you wrote a paragraph describing the physical appearance of the picture?

3. Next to each noun on your list, put down the pronouns you would use to refer to it. For example:

a man in a shirt   he, him, his, it, its

Notice in this example that there are two nouns, each requiring a different pronoun. The proper use of pronouns means the following:

Agreement (with the word to which it refers—in number and person):

The single man thinks he is unseen.
(singular, third person)

The three people have on their party clothes.
(plural, third person)

Correct Case (function of pronouns in sentences):

He (subjective) sees them (objective), but we (subjective) can't be sure they (subjective) see him (objective).

Consistency (sticking to the same number and person):

He walks on by, unseen, ignored. Does he care? Who knows? He may not. He looks like the kind of person who wouldn't.

We can, however, account for changes.

On the other hand, he may be like most people. They don't want to be shunned.

Notice how the words *most people* signal the change here.

Clarity of reference (in tracing the pronoun back to the noun or other pronoun to which it refers):

The three people in line hold their heads high. They look neither left nor right.

Their goes back to *people; they* goes back to *their*.

4. Refer to the "bridge" drawing while completing the following exercises. Correct errors in agreement, case, and clarity of reference.

  a. As he walks by he notices they shoes.
  b. The sea is gray and the sky is white. It provides a nice contrast.
  c. The bridge goes to the horizon. It looks as though the clouds are piled on it.
  d. The man's back is to the viewer. Therefore, you can see the bottom of his shoe as he lifts them.
  e. There is a cloud formation in the background; they extend to the left and right of the bridge.

5. Fill in the correct pronoun.

  a. While he walks along the bridge, _____ hands are in _____ pockets.
  b. He watches each of _____ crowns shine in the sunlight.
  c. The causeway drives into the clouds; once in _____ , _____ disappears from sight.
  d. Where did _____ come from, those people in strange apparel? (Notice that here the word the pronoun refers to *follows* the pronoun itself.)
  e. Only the man _____ could know how important the encounter was, but _____ couldn't know if the others thought _____ equally blessed.

The Introductory Paragraph; Ideas and Concepts; Noun Plurals and Possessives

Write two paragraphs based on the following drawing. In the first paragraph, describe the drawing; in the second paragraph, interpret its meaning. Use plural and possessive forms of nouns correctly.

John Caldwell

The Introductory Paragraph

This writing project calls for a second paragraph, one that interprets the meaning of what we describe in the first. Because the two paragraphs are linked together in this way, the first paragraph now has a new function within the larger structure: it describes the details of the drawing in order to introduce them for later interpretation. From this point on, then, the first paragraph we write will be an introduction.

The introductory paragraph tells our readers what they need to know in order to understand what comes in later paragraphs. We should remember that they do not have us there to answer their questions. Think of their confusion, for instance, if they had not heard of the bat in the "Cupid" drawing (Interproject, p. 35) until our second paragraph. The meaning of the relationship between the bat and Cupid would have been unclear because the connection between the two had not been described earlier.

The introductory paragraph announces what must be interpreted later in the composition. In a composition based on the "Cupid" drawing, for instance, we have to discuss the meaning of the relationship between Cupid and the bat if we described both characters and their connection in the first paragraph. But if we have omitted the bat, we are not entitled to discuss it later. In this way, the introductory paragraph works for the second paragraph as the characterization of a topic sentence (see Writing Project Two, pp. 26–28) works for the body of the paragraph it begins.

We can now adopt the descriptive methods we learned in Writing Project Two as necessary principles of composition. These can guide us in writing introductions and, as we will see later, other parts of the essay as well. These principles are:

1. We must give a full report of the subject matter (*details*).
2. Our readers' need for clarity demands an orderly presentation (*order*).

3. The connections between objects, events, and people must be shown if the meaning of the subject matter is to become clear (*relationships*).

For our introduction to this composition, John Caldwell's drawing presents at least as many details as the preceding drawings did, and with every opportunity to adopt the above writing principles.

> **STEP 1** **From your observation of the drawing, compile a list of details that describe its physical appearance. Try to include every detail. Then group the details and decide on the order best suited to their presentation. (Once again, with two main objects, you have to decide which is most surprising or most important: leading up to it will hold interest.) As a follow-up to Writing Project Two, next to each noun on your list write the appropriate singular or plural pronoun in the subjective case.**

From our past writing, we already know what the topic sentence for a descriptive paragraph looks like. But since introductions to later compositions will possibly describe nonvisual materials, we should make a list now of the functions of topic sentences of introductory paragraphs in general.

1. The *topic* names and provides essential information about whatever is "given" to us: image, idea, object, situation, person, and so on.
2. The *characterization* makes a general statement about one aspect of the topic. In it, we characterize the topic's physical appearance, nature, background, setting, function, or interest.

Generally speaking, we will always be *describing* appearance, if we use the term *appearance* very broadly, in the introductory paragraph. When in later projects the act of description changes somewhat as the materials themselves change, we will return to a consideration of introductions.

> **STEP 2** **Write the topic sentence for a descriptive paragraph introducing John Caldwell's drawing. Mention both main objects in the drawing. Make a proper selection of details based on the characterization in the topic sentence. Then, referring to the details on your list and keeping the drawing in view, write an introduction for this composition.**

The Interpretation of Meaning and the Second Paragraph

The Interpretation of Meaning

We want to know the meaning of this world and of its parts, but meaning most often does not discover us; we have to look for it, find out where it is, if we want to interpret it for ourselves and others. When Alec Guinness, in *Star Wars*, flashes a half-smile and allows his enemy to slay him in a duel, it is up to moviegoers to understand first why he surrenders (the movie only partially explains this), and second what the virtue of surrender in general is. That is, in *Star Wars* we are given the event, but we need to discover a meaning that goes beyond it.

We discover such meanings in everyday life, for example, when we see people slap their foreheads with the palm of their hand. To comprehend such an act, we move away from its literal quality as self-punishment and see it as a sign of someone's having made a stupid mistake or perhaps having forgotten something. This recognition (which we share with others, and which is part of our culture) is our *idea* of what the act means.

Other kinds of knowledge can also lead us to such ideas of meaning. In the drawing for Writing Project Two, for example, we see at first only covered wagons and a particular city. But we know that covered wagons are historically associated with the westward trek of American pioneers, and so we can envision them as representative of that migration. And we know also that the city pictured in the drawing is, if not New York itself, at least what New York represents: the modern American city. The *idea* of the drawing is what we make of the meeting of that migration and that city.

In interpreting both slapping one's forehead and the "wagon" drawing, we perform several functions:

1. We try to go beyond the narrow limitations of what is literally true about them and find a broader application (not just covered wagons but their place in history). Their *particular* nature is less important to us than their *general* nature (not just *these* covered wagons but all covered wagons).
2. We try to discover their *symbolic* quality (covered wagons can stand for pioneer life). We are no longer involved only with concrete details (slapping the forehead or the wagon),

but now can consider those details *abstractly*. (*Migration* itself is an abstract term: the original physical act of moving west is now much less physical and much more an idea.)

When looking for meaning, then, we think in general, symbolic, and abstract terms: we move from the particular, the literal, and the concrete to an idea about them. One way to think and move in this manner is by asking questions about the materials from which we start. If we think about the "bridge" drawing in the second Interproject for instance, we might ask the following questions:

1. What is there about the man walking alone that reveals his mood at the moment?
2. Is there some sort of contradiction between his mood and the appearance of the other people on the bridge?
3. Do the costumes of those people set them apart in history from the solitary man?
4. Do we generally expect, because of the time we live in, that other people will act and dress in one way rather than in another?

In answering these questions (number 3 is obvious but necessary to ask), we have to consider the relationship between the main objects in the "bridge" drawing—the man and the trio. Between the covered wagons and the city, and between slapping one's forehead and looking pained, the relationships are also important. We now can turn again to the present writing project.

STEP 3   Answer the following questions to begin interpreting John Caldwell's drawing:

a. Does the size of the question mark in the drawing matter?
b. Other than its size, is there anything unusual about the nature of the question mark?
c. Does the man's physical connection to the question mark say anything about what it means in his life?
d. What does the man's facial expression indicate about his own view of the situation?
e. Would it affect your interpretation if the man were attached to some other punctuation mark?

The answers to the above questions can be kept in reserve. They will contribute to an understanding of human beings that is based on the "question mark" drawing but that goes beyond the general idea we have of the drawing itself. This same process—the movement from a narrow meaning to a broader one—is made possible by the "bridge" drawing. One general idea we might derive from this drawing is that the man walking alone has a strange and no doubt unexpected meeting. That idea is based on our earlier description of the drawing's physical appearance. It is an idea of the actual event in the drawing, involving the actual characters, not an attempt to discover what these characters and their meeting represent. But such a symbolic meaning is there—in the "bridge" drawing, in the "question mark" drawing, and in all the starting materials in this book. We can discover symbolic meaning by starting from a more limited idea and then moving in the directions of universality and totality:

Universality   Does the idea we have apply to all people? Or does it apply to everybody in a certain group or class? Can we say, for instance, that the meaning of one of the drawings we have described is not limited to its specific character or events but applies to many people in a similar situation or to many such events?

Totality   Is our idea part of a larger whole? For instance, the encounter with people of a bygone age (Writing Project Two) can lead us to consider the meeting between past and present.

When we move in the directions of universality and totality, we produce a concept, such as "the difficulty we all have in separating past and present." To produce a concept for the "bridge" drawing, we can ask the following questions:

1. Can the man in the drawing represent all of us?
2. Since we have referred to the appearance of the royal trio as unexpected, can they symbolize "unexpectedness" itself? Just what produces the unexpectedness we find in them? Is it only the way they are dressed?

It is always possible, of course, to avoid extending the immediate meaning of an object or event (our idea of it) into its wider meaning (a concept); but, unless we do extend meaning, we will not grasp what we have sought after. Concepts enable us to draw mental rings around large areas of experience. For instance, a conceptual understanding of the "bridge" drawing could be that we are always meeting unexpected situations in life; or, it could be that we often encounter the past in the present. If we pay attention to the pastness of the trio, we now have *two* possible ways of understanding. Both refer to people in general, and each refers to the particular concept in question—the unexpected, the past. That is, a certain range of interpretations is possible. No doubt we could arrive at other concepts with regard to this drawing, but not *all* concepts are possible, only those built on the relationships found in the drawing and on an immediate idea of their meaning.

We now can ask ourselves more questions about John Caldwell's drawing.

STEP 4   Answer the following questions in order to understand the full meaning of the drawing for this project:

a. **Can the character in the drawing represent humankind? (To answer this question, we would have to consider his appearance and his relation to the question mark. Also, we would have to think about the particular nature of the question mark: what it represents and what all question marks represent.)**
b. **Can this one question mark represent all question marks?**
c. **What can all question marks symbolize?**
d. **If the character represents humankind, and if the question mark is symbolic, can you produce a statement about their relationship? Such a statement can supply the answers to these questions. Draft this statement now.**

STEP 5   Reexamine your introductory paragraph. Is your description complete enough for an audience who cannot see the drawing but has read your statement of meaning? If, as a result of this reexamination, you think the description is not full or clear enough, make the necessary changes before going on to write the second paragraph.

The Second Paragraph

The topic sentence for our second paragraph might communicate the concept we have just produced.

Since the drawing is the topic of the first paragraph's topic sentence, it would be unnecessarily repetitive to use it again in the topic sentence for the second paragraph. And yet we do want to make a connection between the two paragraphs to show that they both have to do with the drawing, even though they perform different functions. What follows is one way to link the two paragraphs:

1. Review the characterization of the first topic sentence. What can we use from this in our interpretation in the second paragraph?
2. Rephrase what we have chosen.
3. Use this as the topic of the second topic sentence.

	Topic (Drawing)	Characterization (Appearance)
First paragraph		
	Topic (Appearance)	Characterization (Meaning)
Second paragraph		

Our topic sentence for the first paragraph about the "bridge" drawing might have been: *This drawing shows a solitary man meeting several other people on a bridge.* For the second paragraph, our topic sentence could begin with the words *The encounter on the bridge* or *This confrontation.* The rest of the topic sentence would characterize the topic by its meaning:

> This confrontation indicates that people are always meeting the unexpected in life.

Using the above diagram again, we can see how this would work for the "wagon" drawing.

	This drawing by Steven Guarnaccia	portrays wagons heading for a city
First paragraph		
	Such a trip ◄	★
Second paragraph		

STEP 6   Return to your first topic sentence for the "question mark" drawing. Decide how much of its characterization you

---

★The characterization of the second topic sentence is left blank in case this drawing is assigned for interpretation.

need to interpret in the second paragraph. Can you leave out either what the man or the question mark represents, or do you want to discuss both? Rephrase what you have chosen for the topic of your new topic sentence.

The purpose of the second paragraph is now established. It will interpret the drawing described in the first paragraph. As we write this paragraph, it is possible to refer to the first paragraph to show how the objects mentioned in it and their relationships to each other reveal the meaning on which we have decided. But this is probably something we want to do in a limited way, making sure we write mainly about our ideas and concepts themselves. We can use these ideas and concepts to broaden our view of what it is to be a human being and to relate to other human beings. If we return just to a discussion of the drawing, our concerns will probably grow narrower.

We should notice that we have not used a question in any of the topic sentences. Though asking a question is a good device for catching attention, not the question but the answer to it will be the topic sentence:

> What does this encounter tell us? We learn that people are always meeting the unexpected in life.

STEP 7 **Draft a topic sentence for the second paragraph on the "question mark" drawing. Use your work in previous steps as the basis for the topic and the characterization.**

The movement from first characterization to second topic is, as we have seen, a way to keep the composition as a whole from going off the track. But another danger is that the composition can become too mechanical. Later on, when our writing has become more fluent, we should regard the method outlined above chiefly as an underlying organizational principle. The principle is to find a way to connect the subject of one paragraph with the subject of the preceding paragraph. Later, we may not have to do a literal rewording. At this point, it would be advisable to hold very strictly to this method.

In applying the method, we can also use the words *this, that, these* and *those* (*demonstrative pronouns*) at the beginning of the second topic sentence to refer to the first paragraph. We see this done in the following topic sentence:

This encounter indicates that people are always meeting the unexpected in life.

This can be used to refer to *encounter* only if the whole first paragraph has described the meeting; otherwise, it would not be clear that *this* points back to the meeting.

> **STEP 8 Return to the draft of your topic sentence and, if possible or appropriate, revise it to make use of *this*, *that*, *these* or *those*. Write a final topic sentence.**

Having written a second topic sentence for the "question mark" drawing, we now must decide what to put into the second paragraph itself. In deciding, there are two points to keep in mind. One is a reminder: the characterization of the topic sentence dictates what goes in and what stays out of the paragraph. The other point is that the discussion in the second paragraph shows the abstract relationship between the objects in the drawing. In this drawing, the objects concretely linked are the man and the question mark. By stating their connection and their symbolic meaning, we would move from the concrete (description of appearance) to the abstract (interpretation of meaning).

> **STEP 9 Based on the work you did in STEP 4, note whatever details or ideas that support, develop, and illustrate your topic sentence for the second paragraph. In particular, your notes should answer the questions *What?* or *Why?***

Noun Plurals, Related Pronouns, and Possessives

Plurals

The second paragraph of the composition for this project will probably require us to talk generally about people and what happens to them rather than about one person and one event at a time. This will hold true whenever we broaden our interest to include ideas and concepts. In these cases, we will use more noun plurals than before. And since we will often be referring to the thoughts, emotions, attitudes, and behavior that the people possess, we may find a greater use for the possessive case of nouns.

This does not mean, of course, that we have not already had a use for both plurals and possessives when writing description. A description of the "wagon" drawing, for instance, would have been confusing unless we had referred to *oxen* when we meant more than one *ox*, and to *buildings*, not to *building*.

The two kinds of plurals are *regular* and *irregular*. Regular plural endings add *-s*, *-es*, or *-ies* to the singular noun. For the "wagon" drawing, we would use *-s* to make plural *wagons, wheels, horns, buildings*. The *-es* is added to many nouns ending in *-o*, *-ch*, and *-sh*. For example, the pioneers who traveled in covered wagons are often regarded as *heroes*. The character in the drawing for this project is in the *clutches* of the question mark. Describing the "bridge" drawing, we would refer to the *arches* of the bridge. To make plurals of nouns ending in a *-y* preceded by a consonant, we change the *-y* to *-ies*. Comparing the *sky* in one picture to the *sky* in another, we would write *skies*.

Irregular plural endings are exceptions to the various kinds of *-s* endings. *Oxen* is one example of a noun (*ox*) whose plural cannot be predicted from a general rule, even though the *-en* ending for plural is also present in *women* and *children*. One irregular plural we might have use for in this composition is *feet* (from *foot*). Other irregular plurals differ as much as *geese* and *alumni*. A good dictionary lists the plural ending of any irregular noun; when in doubt about the plural of a word, we should look it up.

STEP 10   **Looking at the "question mark" drawing, at your introductory paragraph, and at your notes for the second paragraph, check to see that you correctly used the plural form of any noun when that form was called for.**

Related Pronouns

We often signal our readers that a particular noun is plural by using one of the following words: *all, both, many, some, a few, most, any, several,* and all numbers over one. (It should be noted that these words are only pronouns when they are used as subjects and objects in a sentence. When they directly precede a noun, they are adjectives. In either case, they frequently signal plurals.)

Not all of the arches in the bridge are visible.

Some of the wagons are not pictured.

We must always look beyond our signals, though, to check the way we want them to work in a sentence. These words can also be used with singular nouns:

> Not all of the bridge is visible.

> Some of the wagon train is not pictured.

We must also look beyond our own speech. In speaking, we often use *anyone, anybody, anything*, and the same compounds of *every, some,* and *no* as plurals. In written language, these are singular:

> Nobody seems to be driving the wagons.

> Everyone on the bridge is taking his or her time.

Though we know there could be more than one driver, and though we know there are four people on the bridge, in the above sentences the people are referred to **one at a time.** The same holds true for *none, each,* and *every*—in written language they are always singular:

> Each has a crown on his or her head.

> None of the wagons has a driver.

We should notice in this last example that *none*, not *wagons*, is the subject of the verb *has*. (*Wagons* is the object of the preposition *of*.)

> **STEP 11   Return again to your introductory paragraph. Check to see if you have used any of the pronouns discussed above. If you have, check the number they show (singular or plural). Make sure all pronouns agree in number with the noun or pronoun to which they refer.**
>
> **Each has a crown on his or her head.**

Possessives

There are several ways to show possession when using nouns. One is by saying something *belongs* to something or someone else; another is by using the preposition *of*, as in *the buildings of the city*. These methods can be useful, but often they waste words and confuse meaning by putting the thing owned too far away in the sentence from who or what owns it.

> The buildings of the city are all skyscrapers.

A less clumsy and quite natural alternative to *belongs* or *of* is the use of the *apostrophe*:

> The city's buildings are all skyscrapers.

There are two steps to take in forming the possessive:

1. Establish the singular or plural form (whichever you want to make possessive) of the noun:

   city   singular   *cities*   plural

2. Add one of two possessive endings: apostrophe followed by -*s* to show singular possessive, or -*s* followed by apostrophe to show plural possessive.

   city's   singular possessive
   cities'   plural possessive

For irregular plurals, the apostrophe follows the last letter of the plural form, and the -*s* follows it:

> women's   oxen's   children's

STEP 12 **Review your use of the apostrophe and possessives in your introductory paragraph. If you did indicate possession in any sentence, first see if your noun is singular or plural; then check the possessive ending against the above models.**

STEP 13 **Write a sentence to follow the topic sentence for the second paragraph. See if you can use a plural possessive in your second sentence. Then write a third sentence; in it, try to use a possessive pronoun (refer if necessary to the chart on p. 31) that refers to the plural possessive in the second sentence. For example:**

a. **The encounter on the bridge indicates that we are always meeting the unexpected in life.**
b. **Sometimes the unexpected can be people's unusual ways of dressing.**
c. **For instance, their clothes may be very modern or they may be very old-fashioned.**

STEP 14 **Using your notes and the sentences you wrote for STEP 13, compose the rest of your paragraph. Remember that you have already described the physical appearance of the picture; there is no need to repeat any of its details here. When you finish, review your paragraph for correct use of both plu-**

rals and possessives. Read through both paragraphs of your composition from beginning to end. If you have followed all the steps of this project and are satisfied that you performed each step correctly, your composition should be complete. If for any reason it does not seem that way to you, return to the first step and work your way back through the series of steps by checking your own writing against them.

Interproject | *Exercises and Review*

EXERCISES

1. Try to think of several human gestures or actions, similar to slapping one's forehead, that have meaning beyond themselves. Form an idea of what each gesture means, and then try to produce a concept based on your idea.

2. At the end of each of the following sentences write the concept or concepts that emerge from the sentence. Look back, while you do this exercise, at the drawings to which the sentences refer. For example:

> He swings his shoulders while he walks.
>
> Concept: masculinity.

  a. We don't know what's at the end of the bridge.
  b. The bridge seems to go on forever.
  c. He walks along easily, his hands in his pockets.
  d. It looks as if the pioneers will not reach the promised land.
  e. They never expected to see a modern city.
  f. The city's buildings strike the sky.
  g. Cupid has hit the wrong target.

3. Following the steps for the interpretation of meaning as outlined in this writing project, write a second paragraph for the "bridge," the "Cupid," or the "wagon" drawing. If you choose the "bridge" or "Cupid" drawing, first make sure to write an introductory paragraph if you haven't already done so. If you choose the "bridge" drawing, produce an interpretation different from the one used as an example throughout this writing project. Any of these drawings can be considered alternate assignments for this project.

4. Write the possessive form for the following singular nouns. Then change the possessive singulars to possessive plurals.

    a. bridge   f. person
    b. man   g. sash
    c. dress   h. pants
    d. shadow   i. wife
    e. arch   j. woman

5. Compile a list of details for the "Cupid" drawing. Change all the plural forms of nouns to singular, and all the singular forms to plurals.

6. Correct the following sentences for the use of plurals. One sentence here does not contain an error. While you work, look at the drawings to which these sentences pertain; make certain that what is plural in the drawing is shown to be plural in these sentences. For example:

The man has shoe on.   The man has shoes on.

   a. The city has many building.
   b. Some of the window seem very narrow.
   c. The cloud stretch across the horizon.
   d. How many arch there are is not quite discernible.
   e. Each person in the trio has his or her own sash.
   f. Both of Cupid's wing are as fluffy as his hair.
   g. His arrow are in their quiver.
   h. The bat, as shown by a few line above its head, falls to earth.

7. For practice, return to the passage you wrote in Writing Project One and make all the nouns you used in it plural. Anticipating future writing concerns, try to see what verb changes are necessary now that the subjects of the verbs are changed in number.

8. Change the following to the apostrophe form of the possessive. For example:

The shoes of the man   The man's shoes are
are lumpy.   lumpy.

   a. The buildings belonging to the city penetrate the sky.
   b. The horns of the oxen are as sharp as knives.
   c. Because the hands of the man are in the pockets of his pants, he stands out in contrast to the costumes and decorations worn by the trio.
   d. When the cap explodes, the ears of the rabbit perk up.
   e. The wings that bats have look very different from the wings of the child.

Applying Skills

As we move from one writing project to the next, we take along with us the skills we have already learned. These skills we continue to put to use while learning yet new ones. By the last project, we ought to be fully equipped to write well—that is, if we have developed our writing skills and, in the meantime, forgotten nothing we have learned. But that is the question to ask ourselves: have we kept everything? At this point, let us pause to see if we have.

We can probably do this best by applying these skills to a new piece of writing. When this composition is completed, we should be able to see how much we have learned so far. If that turns out to be less than it should be, then obviously we should return to earlier writing projects for further review.

We can use the following drawing, or the drawing at the end of this project, as the basis for a review composition.

Jo Teodorescu

The first paragraph should describe the drawing; the second paragraph should interpret its meaning. As a reminder of the skills we are trying to make full use of, here is a list with suggestions for how to employ them in this composition.

1. *Basic, compound, and complex sentence forms*
   a. The basic sentence makes a very simple and clear statement; it would work as the topic sentence of the introductory paragraph.
   b. The compound sentence balances equal parts; it could easily be used as part of the description of the characters in the drawing since, as they walk apart, they are taking identical and equally important actions.
   c. The complex sentence subordinates one part to the other; it could be used here to describe what is happening to the cat in Jo Teodorescu's drawing and, at the same time, to indicate how different that event is from normal events.

2. *Description*
   The details having to do with the cat are particularly important to relate. Ordering these and other details in the drawing is difficult because the characters are taking the same action; therefore, there is no special reason to begin with one character or the other. Perhaps the part of the cat you consider most important will determine the order.

3. *Topic Sentence*
   The characterization for the first paragraph's topic sentence should describe the relationship between the two characters in the drawing.

4. *Pronouns*
   Since each character is carrying part of the cat, the possessive case of pronouns will be especially useful.

5. *Noun Plurals and Possessives*

An interpretation that discusses people in general instead of one person at a time will no doubt make it necessary to use noun plurals. Notice that the plural forms of *man* and *woman* are irregular. Showing possession by combining the -*s* and the apostrophe will be useful to indicate what belongs to the man and the woman, and to the groups of people they represent.

6. *Linking paragraphs by topic sentences*

Rewording the relationship between the two characters should provide the topic for the topic sentence of the second paragraph.

7. *Interpretation of meaning*

For this drawing, we will probably want to discuss our idea of what a certain *class* or *group* of human beings is like under certain conditions. We therefore may not need to return, in the body of the second paragraph, to the individuals we have described in the first paragraph. At the same time, it may be useful to refer briefly to them again in order to clarify meaning and to remind our readers of the source of meaning.

The following chart sums up the movement from starting materials (drawing, situation, and so on) to description to interpretation.

Starting Material	*Description*	*Interpretation*
1. Details	literal (cat)	symbolic (what cat stands for)
2. Relationship	particular (*this* man, *this* woman)	general (class or group)
	concrete (the physical act of dividing up the cat)	abstract (the meaning of this action)

We should remember, just as with past writing, to go step-by-step through the composing process. The main steps—those common to all writing projects—are the following:

1. Observe the starting material carefully.
2. Collect, group, and order details.

3. Compose a topic sentence for the introductory paragraph and make a proper selection of details.
4. Write the first paragraph.
5. Compose the topic sentence for the second paragraph.
6. On the basis of the introduction's description of details and the relationship between them, take notes on your interpretation of the drawing's meaning.
7. Write the second paragraph.

Shortly, there will be new steps to learn. But the final step of this and of every composition is to edit, revise, and rewrite what is now on paper. The following Interproject discusses these procedures. Since one of the exercises in the Interproject is to make whatever changes are necessary in this composition, your instructor may not wish for the composition to be turned in until those changes are made.

Interproject | *Editing, Revising, and Rewriting*

The following drawing is an alternative for this review project.

Making Changes

By this time, we may see the need to make changes in our writing before we let it out of our hands. Very possibly, we may not feel completely satisfied with what we have already done if we have simply done it and let it stand. Our dissatisfaction can be healthy.

Whether an amateur or a professional, no writer performs perfectly the first time around. Many writers make grammatical slips; some writers accidentally leave out important points; others get everything backward, and have to start over from scratch. To solve these problems, writers *edit* their work by making corrections; they *revise* by adding, subtracting, or substituting what they need to; and they *rewrite* by producing new content and/or organization. A piece of writing, therefore, can go through several *drafts* before it is fit to be read.

The primary need of our audience is to understand, easily and quickly, what it reads. For the purpose of **immediate** comprehension, language can be viewed as a code of signals that our readers expect us to use correctly, that is, according to prior agreement. These signals are as elementary as the period that ends a sentence and as advanced as the sentence itself. But elementary or advanced, the signals are what we all use when we write. At this point in our writing experience, we may not know every time we have broken the agreement to use a particular signal in a particular way; but the more writing skills we learn and the more we write, the better we will be able to recognize kept promises and to detect and correct broken ones. Making such corrections, which we will turn to first here, is known as *editing*.

Editing

Because editing requires close attention to the smaller details of language, a systematic approach is necessary if we are to make all the changes called for. The first step in this approach is to make certain that you write your first draft *on every other line*. This will enable you to make changes between the lines instead of copying your writing over in order to correct it. Changing between the lines is especially important, since in making a copy you can be tempted to improve only the neatness of your handwriting.

The next step is to prepare a *checklist* of writing skills and the "errors" (broken promises to readers) that can be made in using these skills. A checklist at this moment would include the following:

Sentence forms Are there any run-on sentences? Any fragmentary sentences? When in doubt, check your sentence by identifying both a subject and a verb. Do the correct word(s) and punctuation join two or more clauses in a compound sentence?

> BEFORE His ankle is chained, he looks unhappy.

> AFTER His ankle is chained; he looks unhappy.

For complex sentences, is there at least one clause that does not begin with a subordinating conjunction?

> BEFORE Because his ankle is chained.

> AFTER He cannot move because his ankle is chained.

Pronouns Trace each pronoun back to the word or words to which it refers. Are all the references clear? Have you produced agreement in number and person? Have you used the right case? Has your use of pronouns been consistent?

> BEFORE His feet are planted so firmly on the dot of the question mark that it does not seem it could lose his grip.

> AFTER His feet are planted so firmly on the dot of the question mark that they probably will not lose their grip.

Noun plurals Have you added the right plural ending? Does the noun take a regular or an irregular plural ending? You can sometimes distinguish those nouns that are supposed to be plural by finding a signal word or words that indicate this.

> BEFORE Like the man trapped by the question mark, people have many doubt.

> AFTER Like the man trapped by the question mark, people have many doubts.

Possessives Have you added *both* the apostrophe and the -*s* (for singulars) or just the apostrophe (for plurals) to show ownership? Are you sure you are not using the possessive case when you want only the plural form?

BEFORE No ones question's about life are easy to answer.

AFTER No one's questions about life are easy to answer.

Return to the first sentence of your composition and begin to make every necessary correction. Match each sentence in your composition against this checklist. For each correction in a line, put one check mark in the margin:

√ No one s questions about life are easy to answer.

At the end, return to each line next to which you have put a check mark. See if the change you have made necessitates other changes. For instance, if you had written *this man* and then changed the *this* to *these*, you now would have *these man*. You must go on to change *man* to *men*, since *these* has forced the noun following it to be plural. "Forcings" of this sort happen when we make a correction and then look ahead in the sentence. Sometimes, however, we must look back from a correction. If, for example, we had changed *man* to *men*, but left *this* as it is, we would have *this men*, which is incorrect. In this case, we have to go back from the point of correction and make all the necessary changes in previous writing. Here, we would change *this* to *these*.

Revisions

Editing is the first stage of making changes. *Revising* is the next stage. When we revise, we are concerned with larger units of writing than when we edit; we also may try to improve the *style* of our writing in order to be more exact or to produce greater variety. So far, we have learned several skills whose use we can revise:

Topic Sentence Is there one topic sentence? Does it contain a topic and a characterization? Does the characterization mention only one aspect of the topic? Are you certain the topic sentence for the second paragraph does not repeat the topic of the previous paragraph?

BEFORE (second paragraph) We live in doubt, and life is very hard.

AFTER (second paragraph) The man imprisoned by the question mark tells us that we live in doubt.

Paragraph   The paragraph discusses what the characterization of the topic sentence mentions. Is there any detail or discussion in either of the two paragraphs that belongs in the other one, or in neither one?

Sentence forms   Are the sentences varied in form? Is each form used to do what it does best? For instance, will making two basic sentences into one complex sentence better demonstrate a cause-and-effect relationship?

> BEFORE   The man is wrapped up by the question mark. He can't move.

> AFTER   Since the man is wrapped up by the question mark, he can't move.

Description   Is the detail as complete (or as selective), accurate, and specific as possible?

There are two points to keep in mind at this stage.

1. *If we are somewhat rushed, we should revise first what we consider most important.* On the above list, revising a topic sentence would take precedence over any other revision because the content and organization of the paragraph depend on it so heavily.
2. *Once we revise, we must then go back and edit again.* For instance, if we make the change referred to above—from two basic sentences to one complex sentence—we must make sure the new sentence is punctuated correctly, with a comma after *mark*.

Rewriting

We rewrite when we are so displeased with what we first did—seeing after the fact that this point is dead wrong or that one is misplaced—that there is nothing to do but to do it over. It is not easy, though, to see the need for such radical changes. When we produce our first draft, it is often hard to imagine that it can be improved. Later, we can gain a more objective view of our own work by getting away from it for a few hours or days. When we come back to the composition, we will most likely see it with new eyes.

The steps for rewriting are:

1. Type your composition, using double spaces between lines.

2. Put the composition aside, and not only aside but out of reach and—for a time—out of mind.
3. Return to the composition after enough—but not too much—time has elapsed (you don't want to lose track of what you wrote). You will learn just how long *enough* is after some writing and rewriting experience.
4. Edit and revise; edit the revisions.
5. Rewrite what is necessary. So far our rewriting checklist is brief:
   a. *Description.* Is it necessary to change the *order* in which details are presented?
   b. *Interpretation of meaning.* Does the interpretation now seem wrong in whole or in part?

At the end of each writing and review project, you are responsible for updating your three checklists: editing, revising, and rewriting. Without the new additions, you will not be able to do a complete job.

EXERCISES

1. This review project calls for the application of all skills learned so far. Now it is necessary to test them. Edit, revise, and rewrite (to the extent that any or all of these are necessary) the composition you wrote for this project. Use the checklists in making changes, and follow the steps just outlined.

2. Edit, revise, and rewrite the following paragraphs:
   a. The drawing shows a wagon train. The picture is drawn within a square frame. Several wagon pulled by oxes are heading over a hill. Each wagon is covered by material, no driver are in sight. The city in the left of the drawing is composed of skyscraper. A long road lead's to the city. Because the wagon have wooden carriages and spoked wheels. We can say They are the traditional kinds of vehicle the pioneer used. The city is strange in this picture because it's building comes from a different time. To the left of the buildings there seem to be a factorys smokestacks.
   b. A goat butt's a water-carrier. Making it stumble. A fish escapes from the jar he is carrying. The fish, it looks too big for the jar, it bites the hind leg of a ram. Because, as the

ram butts a bull, the bulls horn both prick one of two baby twin and upset them. One baby twists a legs of a crab. The crab pinches the tail of a lion, as a result the lion roar's at a lady with a scale. She throws up both her arm she screams and drops it. It's pan smacks a scorpion, the scorpion stings a centaur. As that happens, the centaur lets loose an arrow at the goat. Their are stars of different size all over the drawing.

3.   Return to the compositions you wrote in the previous projects. Edit, revise, and rewrite the compositions your instructor asks you to. The changes you make should respond to the comments on your paper. Though you are making changes this time after your compositions have been returned, in the future making changes should precede turning work in.

Developing the Second Paragraph; Illustration by Example; Subject-Verb Agreement

Compose two paragraphs based on the following drawing. (An alternative drawing may be found on p. 89). In the first paragraph, describe the physical appearance of the drawing; in the second paragraph, interpret its meaning. Use illustration by example to extend meaning.

Richard McCallister

We are all concerned, both inside and outside of the classroom, to make clear and accurate connections between persons, events, objects, and ideas. In writing, making connections is a responsibility we have to our readers and also a problem we face in grammar.

One way to show connections in writing is to be careful about agreement between pronouns and the words to which they refer (see Writing Project Two, p. 38):

> The bat's wings spread out as it falls.

It, a singular pronoun, agrees with *bat*, a singular noun.

Another way to show connections is to make one word plural to agree with another plural (see Writing Project Three, pp. 51–53):

> There are several wagons but no drivers visible.

Drivers owes its *-s* to *wagons*.

A third way to make connections is by putting the verb in the singular form if the subject is singular, and in the plural form if the subject is plural:

> The animals in Rube Goldberg's diagram bring it to life.

The verb *bring* connects with *animals* and confirms the fact that more than one animal inhabits the diagram. If there were only one animal, the verb would be *brings*.

In Richard McCallister's drawing of fish for this project, making subjects and verbs agree in number is important if we want to indicate how many fish we are describing at one time. This is a special problem here, because the word *fish* is both the singular and the preferred plural form of the noun (instead of *fishes*), and frequently our readers may have to depend on the verb alone for guidance. In any composition, the readers' acceptance of an interpretation in the second paragraph depends on the writer's clarity in the first paragraph. And often, as is here the case, a clear description depends on subject-verb agreement.

Subject-Verb Agreement

Subjects and verbs must agree in number. For the most part, because of the nature of verb forms, this agreement is only a problem when we write about what is happening in the present. Here is the practice to follow. An -*s* ends a verb in the present tense when the subject is third person singular (*he, she, it,* or any word to which these pronouns could refer.)

We see the practice of ending a verb with -*s* in the following sentences based on past and present drawings:

> The question mark wraps around the man.

An -*s* ends *wraps* because the subject, *question mark*, is the third person singular (*it*), and the verb tense is the present.

> The question mark's coils encircle the man.

No -*s* ends the verb *encircle* because, even though the subject *coils* is the third person, and even though the tense is present, the subject is plural (the *coils*).

> No one fish bears a particular identification, such as a fin in a special place might give it.

Bears is used in this example because the subject is a single fish, as we see signaled first by *no one* and confirmed later in the sentence by the pronoun *it*.

We see in *might give* an exception to the general practice. An -*s* ends neither *might* nor *give* even though third person singular *fin* is the subject. In addition to *might*, there is no -*s* on *must*, *may, can, ought, should, would* and *could*, and no -*s* ending any verb following one of these.

> **STEP 1** **List and group the details in Richard McCallister's drawing. These details will be included in the introductory paragraph. Write out your details in sentence form, remembering to use *fish* for both the singular and the plural. In your sentences, try to use such signal words as *a, all, several, some, every, each, these,* and *none*. Keep in mind that subject-verb agreement is necessary to distinguish one fish from another, and that this is a particular problem in reporting size and position.**

As we have seen, to make verbs agree with subjects we must first recognize a particular subject as singular or plural. Here are six occasions when recognition can be a problem:

1. **Compound subject (see Writing Project One, p. 6).** A compound subject is two or more subjects, joined by *and*, that take the same verb. The verb must be in the plural form.

   The wagon train and the city look strange together.

   City and *wagon train* together make a plural; therefore, *look* is also plural. The following sentence—a very common construction—does *not* contain a compound subject, however, since *as well as* is not a substitute for *and*:

   The city, as well as the wagons, is nicely drawn.

   Singular *city*, not plural *wagons*, is the subject of *is*.

2. **Beginning a sentence with *here* or *there*.** When *here* and *there* occupy the position of the subject in a sentence, the verb still must agree with the real subject, which is always located elsewhere in the sentence:

   Here are several fish facing the same way.

   There is one fish turned around.

   In the first sentence, the subject is *fish*. *Several* signals that *fish* is plural, and so the verb is *are*. In the second sentence, *one* signals that the subject, *fish*, is singular; therefore, the verb is *is*.

3. **Words intervening between subject and verb.** Words intervening between the subject and the verb do not change the number of the subject. Often, these words form prepositional phrases, and it must be remembered that nouns following prepositions (*by, with, in, on, from, to, at*) are always objects, never subjects:

   The buildings in the city form a wedge.

   One of the wagons drawn by the oxen moves forward.

   In the first sentence, *buildings* is the plural subject of *form*. *City* cannot be the subject, because it is the object of the preposition *in*. In the second sentence, *moves* is in the singular form. Though *wagons* and *oxen* are both plural, they are within prepositional phrases; *One* is the subject of *moves*.

4. **Either-or and neither-nor.** In a sentence containing *either* or *neither* in front of one subject and *or* or *nor* in front of

the other, the verb always agrees in number with the subject nearest it:

Either the smallest fish or the next smallest one has to give in.

It seems neither the city nor the wagons belong to the same picture.

The singular subject *one* in the first sentence takes a verb in the singular form. *Wagons,* the subject nearest to the verb in the second sentence, takes a verb in the plural form.

5. *Collective nouns.* Collective nouns like *train* or *group* take a verb in the singular form when they refer to a whole unit and not to its parts:

The wagon train is partly visible.

The group of buildings stands close together.

Train, in the first sentence, refers to all the wagons together and therefore takes *is,* a singular verb. Likewise, *group* collects the different buildings under one name and takes the singular verb *stands.*

6. *Singular subjects in plural form.* A noun may appear to be plural but in actuality be singular.

The news from the smallest fish is probably unwelcome.

Though *news* ends in -*s,* it is singular; *is* agrees with it.

With both the details of the "fish" drawing's physical appearance and whatever combined subjects and verbs from STEP 1 that prove useful, we should now be ready to write an introductory paragraph for this project.

> **STEP 2**   **Write a topic sentence for the introductory paragraph. Then select the appropriate details from your list and decide on the order in which you will present them. If the details are to increase in importance, their order ought to be such that you *end* the paragraph with a mention of the main relationship that exists between the fish. Write the introductory paragraph.**

Before writing the second paragraph, we have to decide several points. One point is the interpretation of the drawing's meaning and how to extend that meaning. The other point is the form we use for the second paragraph.

The Interpretation of Meaning

As we have seen in previous projects, each interpretation we make has to solve a particular set of problems. Part of the difficulty in this drawing is that McCallister's fish represent an abstract idea that does not involve marine life. The fish probably do involve—just as animals do in Aesop, the Brothers Grimm, and Walt Disney—a human meaning. They are symbolic. To discover their meaning, we must look at the drawing more closely.

STEP 3 **Answer the following questions to interpret the meaning of the "fish" drawing.**

a. **What connections do the fish have to each other? Your introductory paragraph should have made this point.**

b. **Can you translate these concrete connections into abstract terms? (For example, in the "question mark" drawing the man was *concretely* bound and *abstractly* imprisoned.)**

c. **Since fish usually do not travel in a straight line, why does McCallister depict them this way?**

d. **What kind of people behave as the four fish on the left do? What kind behaves as the smallest fish does?**

e. **Does the attitude of the smallest fish show an essential difference between types of people? Would some people, caught in the same situation as the smallest fish, react differently?**

STEP 4 **Write a topic sentence for the second paragraph, keeping in mind the questions you just asked and the interpretation they helped you to formulate. Reword part or all of the characterization of the topic sentence of the introductory paragraph for the topic of this second paragraph. In your topic sentence clearly describe the major relationship shown in the drawing.**

We can now examine one way to extend meaning in the second paragraph.

Illustration by Example

While writing a second paragraph for the "question mark" drawing, it would have been quite natural to use examples to discuss the meaning of the drawing. If we began to state that the man captured by the question mark suggests that we all have many doubts, we could imagine our audience asking, "Doubts about what?" Giving concrete examples—doubts about how we will do in college, doubts about whether we will be successful afterwards in getting a good job—might have been a good way to answer this question.

To enable our readers to "see what we mean," we commonly use examples. It is one method—perhaps the easiest, certainly one of the most natural—by which we can extend meaning and give it a clear direction. To use this method at this point is particularly fitting since examples, like subject-verb agreement, involve the need to make connections. That is, the examples we choose must agree with a particular meaning by illustrating it. We succeed in this task when the same basic relationship follows through from the topic sentence of the first paragraph to the topic sentence of the second paragraph, and from there to the sentence announcing the example. The "bridge" drawing, in which who meets what is the subject matter, can demonstrate this kind of movement from the concrete to the abstract and back to the concrete again.

> Guy Billout's drawing shows a man walking alone who meets a royal trio on a bridge.

> This encounter between people from such wildly different times seems to say that in life we often meet what we least expect.

> One example of the unexpected is when we meet people on the street dressed in strange costumes.

Whether using illustration by examples or any other way to extend meaning, we should always try to continue the relationships we observed in the starting material and described in the introduction.

STEP 5 Try to produce three examples of the meaning of the "fish" drawing as it is stated in the topic sentence of your second paragraph. To make certain that each example applies to that meaning, check that it continues to show the main relationship described in your first paragraph and later included in the second paragraph topic sentence. At this point, write no more than a few words describing each example.

Once we have found examples that will allow our readers to see what we mean, we must further test these examples. We can keep

or discard our choices according to how well they succeed in the
following:

1. *The example must be clear.* One aim of illustration by example is to *clarify* meaning, to make it shine through the
   example itself. Doubt about getting a good job is clear, but
   economic doubt—if simply stated that way—is not. For this
   project, we can ask ourselves if we have clearly exemplified
   what the smallest fish and the larger fish represent.

2. *The example should be familiar.* Many readers do not think
   certain ideas and concepts are within their experience until
   examples drawn from everyday life and language are presented to them. Seeing people in strange costumes, though
   they remain an unexpected sight, is a familiar example in
   our age. When we start with some subject as distant as the
   behavior of fish in a drawing, the examples we choose
   should be especially familiar.

3. *The example should be capable of expansion in detail.* Ideas
   and concepts can become more visible, more easily understood, if they can be worked out in concrete detail. We
   should choose examples, therefore, about which we have
   sufficient knowledge.

**STEP 6 Submit the three examples you have produced to the
above tests. Select one example—the one you think is clearest,
most familiar, and potentially richest in detail—for use in your
composition. Write a sentence announcing this example. This
sentence should immediately follow the second paragraph's
topic sentence. It can begin with the words, "One example of,"
"For instance," "To illustrate this," or any other way you can
think of, so long as you signal that you are introducing an example. Since many examples have limited applicability, you
can make this clear in your sentence. For instance, people in
strange costumes are an unexpected sight when they are met
"on the street."**

We can now approach the problem of developing our example.
This problem is not really different from developing an introductory paragraph, where we describe the drawing or some other starting material. The same principles of composition hold true in interpretation as did in description: *details, relationships,* and *order.*

Developing the Second Paragraph

Details

If we are starting from a drawing (as we have so far), then in the introductory paragraph we describe what we see. In doing so, and without realizing it, we are probably answering unspoken questions: *Who? What? Where? When?* We answer *who?* and *what?* when we say it is six fish in a row; and we answer all four questions when we say it is a meeting between an individual and a royal trio on a bridge in the daytime. (Who? An individual and a royal trio. What? A meeting. Where? On a bridge. When? In the daytime.) The answers we give to such questions provide us with the material we need to develop the descriptive paragraph. In order to discover what to say in our interpretative paragraph, we can add *Why?* and *How?* to this list of pertinent questions.

But in the second paragraph, we are asking ourselves these questions about *meaning,* not about *appearance.* Asking questions about meaning should not present a problem if we direct our questions to each term of the relationship described in the sentence that introduces the example. *Terms* are the main parts of what we want to discuss. Often, one term is the subject of a verb and the other term is the word or words following the verb. The verb, in this case, is the link between the terms. In the following sentence, *we* is the first term; *people on the street dressed in strange costumes* is the second term; and *meet* is the link between them.

> One example of the unexpected is when (1) we meet (2) people on the street dressed in strange costumes.

Whether the details we use in the second paragraph come from what we have observed or from what we have arrived at through mental processes (chemical formulas, for instance), we depend on our own knowledge, experience, and imagination. And always our choice of details can be judged according to their specificity, accuracy, completeness, and proper selection. For the present compostion, we can meet these tests without too great difficulty if our examples are clear, concrete, and familiar.

STEP 7   Compile a list of details to support your example. Ask all the above questions that seem relevant to the relationship shown in the second sentence of your interpretative paragraph.

Relationships

A relationship is the connection that exists between persons, ideas, events, or objects. As we have seen, when speaking of relationships we can isolate their terms and the link between them. In writing, if we have gone into detail about each term, we have done much of what is necessary to make the relationship clear. But we have not succeeded in this task until we also have fully discussed the way in which the terms are connected. In *One example of the unexpected is when we meet people on the street dressed in strange costumes,* the verb *meet* is the link between terms. Discussing how the meeting takes place will demonstrate the concept of unexpectedness. For the present composition, another meeting—the head-on meeting between the smallest fish and the other fish—is a concrete link that we can follow through into the second paragraph.

STEP 8 Make a note of the connection between the terms of the relationship in your second paragraph. Answering the question *how?* might give you that connection.

Order

Just as in the introduction, in the second paragraph we can best order details by leading up to the most important one. That detail might very well be the link between the terms of a relationship, since the way in which terms are joined often gives them their importance.

Covering the link between terms of the relationship may also be a good way to end a paragraph. Other times that link as a last point does not seem final enough, and it becomes necessary to write a separate, concluding sentence. In it, we step back for a moment from the points we have just made and allow our audience a sweeping look at them. An interpretative paragraph based on the "bridge" drawing, telling how costumed people on the street exemplify the unexpected, might end with this sentence:

> The result of such a meeting is that sometimes we are not sure what world we exist in.

Or, since the example we have used is so similar to the drawing, we might write:

> Such a meeting is just as surprising, perhaps, as the encounter between the solitary man and the trio in Guy Billout's drawing.

We should notice that neither of these sentences would probably really summarize the points made in the paragraph. Rather, each concluding sentence would be a comment about the result of the link (the actual meeting) between the terms of the relationship discussed in the paragraph.

> **STEP 9   Order the interpretative details you compiled earlier. Think of a possible concluding sentence for your paragraph and, if you can at this point, write it at the bottom of your list of details.**

A proper order for the details in a paragraph is essential to full comprehension. Yet this order will remain obscure unless the connection between a sentence containing one detail and a sentence containing the next detail is made clear. Although we may know what those connections are, our readers will not until we signal them. The following are ways to signal the connections between sentences:

1. Begin sentences with the single words (coordinating conjunctions) or transitional phrases used to link clauses in compound sentences (see Writing Project One, pp. 7–8).
2. Use *this, that, these* or *those* (*demonstrative pronouns*), making certain that their reference is clear, at or near the beginning of a sentence (see Writing Project Three, p. 50).
3. Use a pronoun at or near the beginning of a sentence to refer to a noun or a pronoun in the previous sentence (see Writing Project Two, pp. 30–31).
4. Repeat one or more words from a previous sentence to establish a point of reference.

> The fish in Rube Goldberg's diagram seem undisturbed. Each fish is swimming peacefully.

Based on the "split cat" drawing in Review Project One, the sentences below demonstrate these methods of connecting sentences. Each connecting word is numbered to correspond to a method:

> Neither the man nor the woman would let go of the cat. Therefore (1), when they (3) broke apart so violently, each of them ended up with one half of the poor animal. Nonetheless (1), in the drawing the cat (4) does not seem too unhappy. It (3) merely looks dazed. This (2) kind of expression also appears on the couple's faces.

STEP 10 Finish the interpretative paragraph for this composition, extending meaning through illustration by example. Look once more at the "fish" drawing to check that your whole composition represents the drawing's physical appearance and meaning. Somewhere in your second paragraph, perhaps in your concluding sentence, you may refer to the fish in the drawing. It is from them, after all, that your composition began.

STEP 11 Edit, revise, and rewrite your composition. Add to your editing checklist subject-verb agreement and connections between sentences. Add to your revision and rewriting checklists the second sentence of the interpretative paragraph (which announces the illustrative example), the concluding sentence of a paragraph, and the methods of connecting sentences within paragraphs. Add to your rewriting checklist illustration by example and ordering interpretative paragraphs.

Interproject | *Exercises and Review*

The following drawing by Guy Billout is
an alternative for Writing Project Four.

Guy Billout

EXERCISES

1. Correct any errors in subject-verb agreement in the following sentences.

> BEFORE Each of the rabbit's paws are in the air.
>
> AFTER Each of the rabbit's paws is in the air.

    a. In the drawing, there is the black crowns of a group of trees. They rise on slender trunks from beyond a stone wall and merges to form a smear as black as ink.

    b. The car bumper curve like a fence around the tires, which resembles dougnuts.

    c. Neither of the two fish seem too concerned about what is happening around them.

    d. One of the three people walking together on the bridge have more authority than the other two has.

    e. The cloud formation hangs over the end of the bridge.

    f. None of the three people are looking at the individual.

    g. The lone man, like most people in his situation, probably do not think he sees what he see.

    h. The man's feet, each of which are almost slipping off the ball, looks too unsteady to hold him up.

    i. Because the tail of the question mark, in several folds, wrap around the man, his arms are pinned to his side. There seem to be no place he can escape to.

    j. The links of the chain leads from the ball to his ankle.

2. Return to the compositions that you have so far written for this course and have received back from your instructor. If any errors in subject-verb agreement have been marked, correct them now. As you do so, refer to both the appropriate pages in Writing Project Four and to the drawing on which your writing was based.

3. Reexamine your past compositions for new and varied ways of connecting sentences. Do your paragraphs have concluding sentences?

4. What is the symbolic value of these famous animals?
    a. Noah's dove
    b. The serpent in the Garden of Eden
    c. The phoenix
    d. The American eagle
    e. The ostrich with its head in the sand

5.   Without mentioning the animals themselves, write a conceptual statement about each of their symbolic values. Make certain to show a clear relationship in each. Then, find an example to illustrate each statement.

6.   Find examples you might use to illustrate the following conceptual statements:
   a. People, like chipmunks, are always scheming to achieve their own ends.
   b. Many people complicate their lives unnecessarily.
   c. For some people, producing complications is fun in itself.
   d. Often when we attempt to escape something, we find it waiting for us.
   e. Between two people who are in love, there is frequently something that comes to spoil their happiness for a while.

7.   Write a paragraph using one of the statements from exercise 5 or 6 above; illustrate your statement with one of the examples you have chosen. For any of the statements in exercise 6, find the drawing on which it is based and keep it in view as you collect, shape, and order your details.

WRITING PROJECT FIVE | **Thesis Sentence; Narration; Conclusions; Verb Tenses**

Compose a full essay (introduction, body, and conclusion) based on the following drawing. (An alternative drawing may be found on p. 109.) Relate your statement of meaning in a thesis sentence. Use narration as a way to extend meaning.

Guy Billout

The first step of the current writing project should be familiar by now.

STEP 1 Collect and group descriptive details. Write a topic sentence for an introductory paragraph that describes the physical appearance of the drawing. Select the proper details and order them; then, write the first paragraph of this composition. You may want to start from the assumption, which close observation might have led you to make on your own, that the two figures in the drawing are representations of the same person at two different times. For your introductory paragraph, this special representation could determine the order of details.

The Interpretation of Meaning

In the "cliff and cloud" drawing for this project, we have to interpret the meaning of each figure separately, and then of the two together. In doing so, we should remember that it is human beings in general, not a character in the drawing alone, with which we are finally concerned.

STEP 2 Answer the following questions about the two figures and their positions:
   a. What does the man's location on the edge of the cliff indicate? Does the fact that he has reached a certain height have symbolic meaning?
   b. What does the man's position on the cloud indicate? What is the symbolic meaning of standing on a cloud?
   c. Can you compare the symbolic positions of the two figures?
   d. What does the difference in size between these two figures indicate? Is there anything else about the different figures that has symbolic value?

e. Can you think of a concept that would name the situation the two figures are in and thus help to state the relationship between them?

STEP 3   On the basis of the answers you gave to the questions in STEP 2, write one sentence interpreting the meaning of this drawing.

The Thesis Sentence

This writing project is the first to call for a full essay. In a full essay, the topic sentence of the second paragraph no longer contains the main statement of meaning. Instead, we have a separate sentence—*the thesis sentence.*

The reason for making this change is that the second paragraph might be joined by a third, a fourth, a fifth, or more paragraphs to produce the body of the essay. Since a topic sentence states only what one paragraph at a time will discuss, we must have a broad statement of meaning that several paragraphs could develop. Each of those paragraphs would have its own topic sentence.

The thesis sentence can be a one-sentence paragraph immediately following the introduction to the essay, or it can be the last sentence of the first paragraph. But wherever it is located, the thesis sentence is exactly what we have so far produced as the topic sentence of the second paragraph. It functions more broadly now,

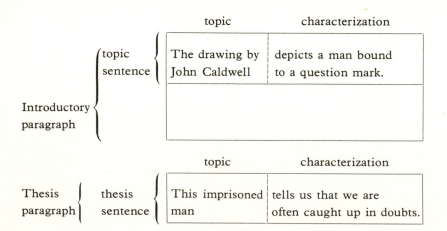

but it still has a topic and a characterization; it is determined by what precedes it, and, in turn, it determines what follows it.

Just as before, we reword the characterization of the topic sentence of the first paragraph: it becomes the topic of the statement of meaning, the thesis sentence.

The characterization of the thesis sentence determines what is to be discussed in the body of the essay:

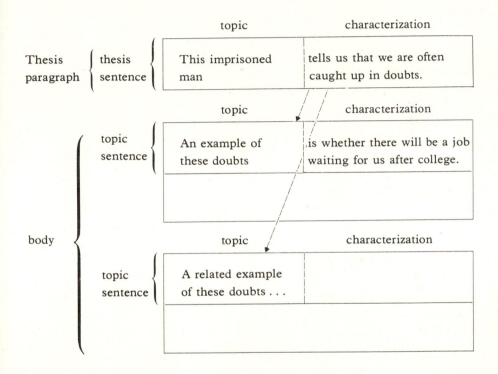

We can see the same movement from topic sentence to thesis sentence to topic sentence in a composition based on the "bridge" drawing:

Topic sentence (introductory paragraph):

Guy Billout's drawing shows a man meeting a royal trio on a bridge.

Thesis sentence (thesis paragraph):

This encounter between people from such wildly different times seems to say that in life we often meet what we least expect.

Topic sentence (body of essay):

> One example of the unexpected is when we meet people on the street dressed in strange costumes.

STEP 4   Based on the work you did in STEP 3, write a thesis sentence for the "cliff and cloud" drawing. In the characterization, try to continue the relationship you described in the topic sentence of the introductory paragraph. Here, of course, this relationship will be in abstract terms.

After moving from concrete description to abstract interpretation, we sometimes use concrete language again to make our meaning visible to everyone. Illustration by example, as we found in Writing Project Four, helps our readers to see meaning. So does another method used to extend meaning, one that is relevant to writing for many college courses—narration.

Narration

"One example of people standing up for their rights," we might have written to illustrate the meaning of the "fish" drawing in Writing Project Four, "is the little guy fighting back against a bully." To develop this example, we might go on to tell a story about such a fight. If we do, our example has become a narrative. To illustrate meaning in this way is one of the chief uses of narration.

A narrative is, first of all, a sequence of events. These events move from one time to another, backward or forward, or backward and forward, depending on how the story is told and who is telling it. Usually, there is a high point within the narrative, a climax that the action moves toward. The narrative can end at its climax, or there can be a winding down of the action after the climax. And, of course, most stories involve characters, especially someone at the center of the action, as we or someone we know might be at the center of a story about resisting a bully.

STEP 5   Think of a narrative for the body of your essay that illustrates your thesis sentence. At this point, note down both the major events of the narrative and some information about the character(s) to whom these actions happen. Try to tell the story as a sequence of events moving from the past to the future.

If the narrative we tell is to illustrate effectively our thesis sentence, it must meet the following standards:

1. The narrative must be relevant. As with illustration by example, a narrative should reflect the relationship derived from the thesis sentence:

THESIS SENTENCE   The situation of the smallest fish tells us that when people have finally had enough they will stand up for their rights.

BODY TOPIC   This happened to me once when I had to fight the neigh-
SENTENCE   borhood bully.

2. The connection between characters and action should be clear.
3. The narrative must add up to something. Either the climax or the winding down of the action, or both climax and winding down, should illustrate meaning.
4. The narrative must not be too short to illustrate the whole of the meaning stated in the thesis sentence. Likewise, the narrative should not be so long that it distracts from its function—to extend meaning.

STEP 6   Check your notes to see if, once told, the narrative would pass the above tests. If it looks deficient in any respect, reshape it now.

A last and most important standard for judging the value of any narrative is how well it shows the passage of time. In the written expression of standard English, verbs are chiefly responsible for indicating time and the movement from one time to another. We cannot actually tell a story that extends meaning without a command of verb tenses.

Verb Tenses

If we were telling a story to explain only the physical actions of the "cliff and cloud" drawing, we could write the following:

The man **had climbed** up the cliff since 2 p.m. Often, he **gave up** hope. But he **told** himself that he **would make** it; and, finally, at 3 p.m. he **reached** the peak. Since then, time **has flown** by. Now he **stands** there, looking at a cloud. For a moment, he **thinks** he **has been** there always. But he **wants** to go on. Tomorrow he **will do** it. By this time next week, he **will** already **have been** on a cloud for a long time.

The emphasized verbs in this paragraph move the character from the past through the present and on into the future. These are the three main divisions of time when we discuss verb tenses: past, present, and future. We can represent all the main forms of the verb by using two verbs from the previous passage as examples: *to reach* and *to fly*.

To reach is a regular verb. That is, both forms of its past tense take the *-ed* ending.

To Reach

Present   reach   *Past*   reached   *Past participle*   reached

To fly is an irregular verb. Its forms of the past tense follow no regular pattern and must therefore be memorized. A good dictionary lists the forms of all irregular verbs.

To Fly

Present   fly   *Past*   flew   *Past participle*   flown

STEP 7 **Return to your notes for a narrative illustrating the drawing for this project. For later reference, identify the various tenses shown by your verbs.**

Now, let us examine the verb tenses, taking them up one by one. In doing so, we will see how the passage on pp. 99–100 was written. Since the narrative that will illustrate the meaning of the "cliff and cloud" drawing may begin, as many narratives do, in the past, we can examine verb tenses by starting furthest back in time and then working our way forward. (Refer to the drawing with each example below.)

Past Perfect: had + past participle (-ed ending)

The *past perfect* is used when we refer to any action that started in the past (2 p.m. in our example) and ended in the past (3 p.m.). We form it by using *had* with the past participle of the verb. For future reference, *been* is the past participle of *to be*.

The man had climbed up the cliff since 2 p.m.

Simple Past Tense

The *past tense* refers to a definite time earlier than the present. Regular verbs use the *-ed* ending to form their past tense. Irregular verbs have independent forms of the past tense.

> Finally, at 3 p.m., he reached the peak.

If we want to talk about what happened to the man *during* his climb, between the hours of 2 p.m. and 3 p.m., we use the past tense (*Gave* is the past tense of the irregular verb *to give*):

> Often, he gave up hope.

Whenever we refer to the past, and then want to refer to an event that will happen after that particular point in the past, we use *would*:

> But he told himself that he would make it.

The passage now reads:

> The man had climbed up the cliff since 2 p.m. Often, he gave up hope. But he told himself that he would make it; and, finally, at 3 p.m. he reached the peak.

STEP 8   Check your notes for use of the two forms of the past: simple past and past perfect.

Present Perfect: have or has + past participle

We use the *present perfect* to show the passage of time from the past up to and including the present. To form the present perfect, we add *has* or *have* to the past participle.

> Since then, time has flown by.

The present perfect can also express a state of being that stretches from the past to the present:

> For a moment, he thinks he has been there always.

Present Tense

The *present* tense describes the here and now. We form it, naturally, by using the present tense form of the verb. In using more or less dramatic prose, such as that on p. 99, we write:

> Now he stands there, looking at a cloud.

We also use the present tense to make statements that are *always* true, not just true at the moment:

> God stands on a cloud in many religious paintings.

Adding the present tense and the present perfect, our passage now reads:

> The man had climbed up the cliff since 2 p.m. Often, he gave up hope. But he told himself that he would make it; and, finally, at 3 p.m. he reached the peak. Since then, time has flown by. Now he stands there, looking at a cloud. For a moment, he thinks he has been there always. But he wants to go on.

STEP 9   Check your notes for use of the present tense and the present perfect.

Future Tense

To refer to a *future* time, we generally use *will* with the infinitive form of the verb (minus the *to*):

> *infinitive form* **to do**   *future tense*   **will do**
> *Tomorrow he will do it.*

We should remember that *will* expresses the future of the present time only, not the future of the past. We move now from *he wants to go on* to what he will do tomorrow.

Future Perfect: will have + past participle

To refer to a time that stretches from the present to some future time, or from the future to a still more future time, we use the *future perfect*. We form the future perfect by adding *will have* to the past participle. This is perhaps the least frequently used form of the verb.

> By this time next week, he will already have been on a cloud for a long time.

The passage, with its verb sequence showing a movement from past to future, is now completed.

> The man had climbed up the cliff since 2 p.m. Often, he gave up hope. But he told himself that he would make it; and, finally,

at 3 p.m. he reached the peak. Since then, time has flown by. Now he stands there, looking at a cloud. For a moment, he thinks he has been there always. But he wants to go on. To-morrow he will do it. By this time next week, he will already have been on a cloud for a long time.

STEP 10 Check your notes for your use of the future and the future perfect.

We are now ready to produce the body of this essay.

STEP 11 Compose the topic sentence for the one-paragraph body of your essay. Link the statement of meaning to the extension of meaning. Do so by adopting what is essential in the characterization of the thesis sentence for the topic of the new topic sentence. It might be helpful to use the conceptual word from your thesis sentence in the new topic sentence.

STEP 12 Using your notes and topic sentence, write the narrative that will illustrate your thesis. Look back to the discussion of verbs in this project as you work. Particularly keep in mind the passage describing the climb made by the character in the drawing. That passage is a model of verb sequence.

A last word about narration and verb tenses: there are other words in the language that reinforce verbs by indicating the time or the stretch of time to which we are referring. For instance, we can refer to a time starting in the past and ending there by saying *up until then* or *before then*. We can substitute *now* for *then* in the above phrases to indicate an action that started in the past and has continued to the present. We can also use *since*, as in *Since then, some time has passed*. The past can be referred to by such terms as *a moment ago*, *last night*, and *in the past*. We can also use *today* in this connection, if by that we mean a time earlier in the day. *At this point*, *at present*, and *right now*, refer to the present. *Tomorrow*, *next week*, and *later on* refer to the future. We should notice that *then* can refer to a later time as well as to an earlier time: *Then, I will be on a cloud*.

STEP 13 Review your narrative for its use of other words sig-nalling time. If they are necessary to make the time referred to clearer for your audience, insert them.

The Conclusion

When we come to the end of a narrative or a composition, we can simply raise our pen from the paper and stop writing; or, we can bring what we have written to a true conclusion. The final part of this writing project is the study of conclusions.

In Writing Project Four (pp. 85–86), we saw that the concluding sentence of an interpretative paragraph tells—more than all else—the result or outcome of that paragraph. A concluding paragraph does the same for the whole essay by performing one of the following functions:

1. *Summary.* In relatively brief essays, like those we are writing, our readers can glance back at the points made in the body, and so a summary of them is often unnecessary. But a summary is often useful as the conclusion of a long essay or term paper. In either of these, the body of the composition could be as long as twenty paragraphs. By the time our readers reached the end of such a composition, they would not have remembered all of those points used to support the thesis sentence. Nor would they remember the order in which those points were presented. A summary neatly solves this problem by tying the points together into a tidy package. One easy way to write a summary is simply to list the main points made in the essay.

2. *Emphasis.* By the end of an essay based on the "fish" drawing (to use it as an example), we might be able to see that fighting back is not only something people do when forced to, but is necessary to physical survival, self-respect, and human dignity. If we can make these points in a conclusion, it is thanks to the full and clear way we extended meaning in the body of the essay. And by making these points, we emphasize the meaning stated by the original thesis sentence by showing our readers a deeper understanding of it. Providing emphasis is especially useful for the conclusions of essays in which we illustrate by example or narrative, conduct an analysis, define a term, or compare and contrast two items.

3. *Significance.* The significance of any meaning is its connection to another idea, situation, event, person, or institution. To make this connection, we should show how our original idea or concept has a broader application than we

have so far indicated. That is, as a result of what we have written, the meaning we have stated earlier can be shown to have entered into the world of other meanings. As a conclusion to the "fish" drawing, for instance, fighting back could be shown to have an important connection to the individual in society, or to particular social groups. When we do approach a conclusion this way, however, we must be careful to keep the relationship between what is in the essay and what is outside of it clear. Otherwise, we could find ourselves writing a new essay altogether.

Though the above functions can be combined in the concluding section of a composition—even within the one paragraph we will conclude with—the brevity of the essays we are writing probably calls for us to emphasize *or* to show the significance of our thesis sentence, but not both.

STEP 14   Decide whether emphasis or significance will be the function of your conclusion by reading over your writing and asking yourself what you have more to say about—the meaning stated by the thesis sentence itself, or something to which that meaning has an important relation. Make notes for your concluding paragraph.

The concluding paragraph, like the introduction and the body of an essay, requires a topic sentence. The topic of this sentence can come from any part of either preceding topic sentences or from the thesis sentence. It depends on where we first want to direct the attention of our readers. We should recall the example used earlier in this chapter:

FIRST TOPIC SENTENCE   Guy Billout's drawing shows a man meeting a royal trio on a bridge.

THESIS SENTENCE   This encounter between people from such wildly different times seems to say that in life we often meet what we least expect.

SECOND TOPIC SENTENCE   One example of the unexpected is when we meet people on the street dressed in strange costumes.

The topic sentence of the third, or concluding, paragraph could refer to the first topic sentence. We might feel that the starting material is important because it was responsible for initiating the thinking process that followed it:

> And so, starting from a picture that shows an unexpected meeting, we now can see that . . .

Or the topic sentence of the third paragraph could refer to the meaning stated in the thesis sentence, because of its dominant position in the essay:

> Meeting the unexpected, as we might have gathered, is . . .

Or, we can refer to the way we extended meaning if we think that what is in the body of the essay is most interesting:

> As we can plainly see in the above example . . .

The characterization of the topic sentence is done by summary, emphasis, or significance. For instance, we could complete the first and third topic sentences listed above by adding the following words:

> . . . meeting the unexpected can be a learning process.

This particular characterization would depend on the particular way in which we developed our example.

For the opening of a concluding paragraph, there are signal words that can be helpful to the audience. Using a term like *in conclusion* is an obvious way to begin, but because it is so obvious and has been used so often, it has little impact. There are other choices—groups of words like *So, as we can see, As we may have gathered by now,* and *What we know from the above discussion.* These enlist the audience in a joint effort to put everything together at the end of the essay. They are less harsh than *in conclusion* and yet give us a certain authority that persuades our readers that the essay truly is concluding.

We go on in the concluding paragraph to support the characterization in the topic sentence by answering one or another question about it. *How?* would be appropriate in our example. (Look back to p. 84 in Writing Project Four for a review of these questions.) To write the paragraph, we apply the compositional principles—which should be quite familiar to us by now—of details, order, and relationship.

STEP 15 Write the topic sentence for your concluding paragraph. Then, on the basis of the notes you made earlier, write the paragraph itself. Do not introduce a new idea or a new story; there is no more room to develop it. And be careful not to end on a detail whose presence here instead of in the body of your essay will startle the reader.

With the full essay now in hand, we can take the last step, which is to make changes where necessary.

> **STEP 16**   Edit, revise, and rewrite your essay. To your editing checklist, add verb tenses. To your revision checklist, add the thesis sentence (with particular attention to the idea that it is a statement of meaning in a new position and with a broader function). Rewriting would be necessary if, upon later inspection, you found the story did not illustrate your thesis sentence.

Interproject | *Using Verbs*

The following drawing by Guy Billout is
an alternative for writing in this project.

Guy Billout

EXERCISES

1. The following narrative, based on the "bridge" drawing, is divided into two paragraphs. The verb tenses in the first paragraph are correct. Identify the tense of each verb. For example:

> the man we now see   present

In the second paragraph, many of the verb tenses are incorrect. Correct them.

> BEFORE his objections done him
>
> AFTER his objections did him

This morning, the man we now see on the bridge woke up feeling his life was about to change. This itself was a change for him. For a long time he had felt he could not make any progress in his life. He could not achieve the goals he had set himself. But in a dream last night he heard himself making the following speech: "No," he said aloud to someone he could not see but whom he felt he had known for a long time. "I'm going places. I'm going to be somebody. I will not always be stuck in a rut."

Of course, his objections done him no good last night; they never have before. But this morning he feels somewhat different about life. Perhaps this is because of the vision he saw this moment as he go across the bridge: three people, two men and a woman, dressed in robes and wearing crowns on their heads. Never has he saw anything like this before. Nor has he know the present so suddenly to give way and produce an image of the past. He is exciting but kept his hand in his pockets to hide his feelings. "What will the future bring," he asked himself, "now that I had seen the past?"

Follow the same procedure for the following two paragraphs based on the "wagon" drawing.

Betsy Ingersoll, originally a Bostonian, left for California with her husband Kenneth. Life in the East did not particularly suit the couple anymore. Prices were high, jobs were scarce, and the city had grown too big for comfort. It was this last point in particular that disturbed the Ingersolls. They wanted space around them, room to grow a garden; they wanted to be able to walk down the street and not have to dodge people coming the other way. True, their friends criticized them for leaving. "You are escapists!" they said. But nothing could change the Ingersolls' minds, and in 1844 they went West.

In August of that year, they cross the Salt Lake Desert. Up to that point, they never saw such a wide stretch of desert. It was dead white and seem to go on forever. They had thought they will never get to its end. At last, however, they make it to the other side, and they realized that their goal is practically in sight. There was no denying that there are mountains still to cross, but in their imaginations they could see the lush greens of California. Or, at least, Mr. Ingersoll had seen them. Mrs. Ingersoll, in the first wagon of the train, has a different vision. She saw a city, more modern than she ever saw before, with tall steel and glass towers that seemed to scrape the sky. The city rises up in front of her. Her vision of it only lasts for a few moments, but in those moments she had grew wise. "No one can really escape anything," she tells her husband, and when he asked her what she is saying, in reply she only took his arm.

2. Most of the following sentences contain errors in verb tenses. Make corrections where it is necessary to do so:

> BEFORE Did someone called him?
>
> AFTER Did someone call him?

a. The bat has been shoted.

b. Last night, he fire an arrow so that someone will fall in love.

c. Cupid probably be hitting the wrong target all night.

d. True, he had knock down a bat, but he had know he eventually will hit the right target.

e. Walking slowly, he made his way across the bridge.

f. Those people have turn out in strange clothes.

g. They representing the past.

h. This is not the first time he has went across this bridge, nor would it be the last, but he know it to have been the most important time.

i. Tomorrow he will try to cross again.

j. Has a city been raise in the desert, or is this a mirage the man had had?

k. Oxen use to pull wagons in those days; they were putted to use because they were cheaper than horses are.

l. The city probably been there for a long time before the wagons arrive.

3. For each of the following sentences, write additional sentences incorporating the original in a very short narrative. Use different verb tenses by shifting into the future and the past. Try to use each verb tense at least one time.

BEFORE He is climbing the mountain.

   AFTER He was sweating in the valley where he had eaten breakfast earlier. Now he is climbing the mountain and for a while has been thinking about his time in the valley. Soon he will reach the top. By tomorrow at this time he will have been there for some time.

a. The cloud will float away with him.
b. His hands were in his pockets.
c. He has been looking straight ahead for ten minutes.
d. He had seen himself lifted from the cliff to the cloud.
e. Was he transporting himself somehow?

4. Practice narration by writing a story (instead of using an example) to illustrate the meaning of the "fish" drawing or the "daisy" drawing in Writing Project Four.

5. Write a conclusion for the composition you have written on either of the above drawings. As an alternative, return to any other composition you have written and compose a conclusion for it.

Paraphrasing; Classification; Comparison and Contrast; Active and Passive Voice; Transitive and Intransitive Verbs

Compose a full essay on either the following drawing or the following narrative. (An alternative drawing may be found on p. 127.) In the thesis sentence, classify the types of people observed in the starting materials. Compare and/or contrast these people in the body of the essay.

William Steig

"Muddy Road"[1]

Tanzan and Ekido were once traveling together down a muddy road. A heavy rain was still falling.

Coming around a bend, they met a lovely girl in a silk kimono and sash, unable to cross the intersection.

"Come on, girl," said Tanzan at once. Lifting her in his arms, he carried her over the mud.

Ekido did not speak again until that night when they reached a lodging temple. Then he no longer could restrain himself. "We monks don't go near females," he told Tanzan, "especially not young and lovely ones. It is dangerous. Why did you do that?"

"I left the girl there," said Tanzan. "Are you still carrying her?"

For this project, the essay may be based on the short narrative "Muddy Road," or on the drawing by William Steig. If the essay is based on "Muddy Road," it will be necessary to describe what happens in the narrative. Doing this may be the initial writing problem. Before now, we have only described diagrams or drawings, but if we keep in mind our approach to describing pictures, we will see that describing words is in many ways similar.

Paraphrasing

A paraphrase, or a short restatement, offers a different and simpler version of an original statement. It puts the original statement in other words. For instance, when a point in the original is made in words that seem very much the creation of that particular writer, in our paraphrase of that point we use words that are as much our

---

[1] From *Zen Flesh, Zen Bones*, a Zen Buddhist anthology edited by Paul Reps. Reprinted by permission of the publisher Charles E. Tuttle Co., Inc., Tokyo, Japan.

own as possible. In a paraphrase of "Muddy Road," we would probably substitute for *lodging temple*; it is unlikely that we would use *lodging temple* in our own writing, and our readers would more easily understand a more familiar term.

Usually a paraphrase puts the original in a different form. This is because immediate understanding is the chief motive. If the original is a narrative, like "Muddy Road," the paraphrase would not use dialogue and dramatic form at all.

Also, the paraphrase covers everything, from beginning to end of whatever whole or partial text it treats.

To a limited extent, we have paraphrased whenever we reworded the characterization of a topic sentence or a thesis sentence to use it as the topic of the next statement of meaning:

TOPIC SENTENCE   Guy Billout's drawing portrays the same man twice.

THESIS SENTENCE
(TOPIC)   This double representation of the figure . . .

In the above topic, *representation* refers to *portrays* and is a different word in a different form, a noun instead of a verb. *Double* refers to *same* and *twice*, and *figure* refers to *man*.

> **STEP 1 (narrative) Paraphrase the first two paragraphs of "Muddy Road." Your paraphrase will probably supply the characterization of a topic sentence for your introductory paragraph. (If your instructor does not assign "Muddy Road" for this project, you may return to the discussion here if you need to paraphrase later on in this book.)**

"Muddy Road" consists of several very short scenes that are easy to visualize; therefore, describing its appearance really is like describing that of a picture. In the future, other texts will probably not be as visual; but to them as well as to "Muddy Road" we can apply the compositional principle of *details, order,* and *relationship.*

The *order* we use in paraphrase is the simplest, most direct, and most straightforward. "Muddy Road" already follows this order; many narratives do not. "Muddy Road" is straightforwardly chronological, and there is no good reason to impose a new order on it if we want to end with the most important point. At other times, however, we might need to rearrange the original order to make the most important point come last.

Relationships—between characters and between events—are necessary to reproduce in a paraphrase. In "Muddy Road," we would need to show the relationships between Tanzan and Ekido, and between them both and the girl.

As mentioned earlier, the *details* we include are those necessary to the understanding of our readers.

> **STEP 2 (narrative)** Write down the details of the narrative. Alongside these details list other words that you might use for them in a paraphrase. Refer to the draft you wrote for **STEP 1** and write a topic sentence for an introductory paragraph.

> **STEPS 1 and 2 (drawing)**   List and group details of the "man and woman" drawing. For the introductory paragraph, write a topic sentence. In the characterization, try to depict the relationship between the man and the woman. Decide whether the man or the woman is more important or interesting. Who will you describe last?

From our observation either of Tanzan and Ekido or of the man and woman in William Steig's drawing, we can say that one character in each pair is active while the other is passive. In writing an introductory paragraph describing the drawing and, to a lesser extent, the story, we can indicate these differences by using one verb form rather than another. Let us look at these forms, then, before going on to write the first paragraph.

More on Verbs (1)

Active Voice

When the subject of a verb moves toward the end of a sentence, that verb is in the active voice:

The man crosses a bridge.

Man as subject acts on the direct object, *bridge*. (A *direct object* answers the question *what?* The man crosses what? A *bridge*.) *Crosses* is in the active voice.

Often, however, the object in a sentence is not direct; instead, it follows a preposition:

The man crosses to the other side.

Side is the object of the preposition *to*. *Crosses* is still in the active voice in this sentence because the subject, *man,* is moving toward the end of the sentence.

A verb in the active voice sometimes takes no object at all:

The man walks.

Passive Voice

When the subjects of verbs are acted upon, the verb is *passive:*

The bridge is crossed by the man.

As we see in the above sentence, the passive voice reverses the order of subject and object: *bridge* is now the subject of the verb; *man* is the object of the preposition *by*.

Or we may write a sentence in which only the former object is present:

The bridge is crossed.

Whichever kind of sentence we produce, the passive voice always joins a form of the verb *to be (am, is, are, was, were)* to the past participle (*-ed* form) of the verb. Or it joins *has, have,* or *had* to *been* and the past participle:

The other side has been reached.

In a sentence where the real subject (the man crossing the bridge) is not mentioned, as in *The other side could have been reached by now,* we may wonder just who it is that may have reached the other side. This is one weakness of the passive voice: it can make the real subject disappear when we need to show responsibility for action. Another weakness is that the sentence—deprived of dramatic movement—is reduced to a statement *about* action.

On the other hand, the strength of the passive voice is its ability to do justice to some situations. We can see this in the following sentence:

The man is trapped by the question mark.

Here, the reality of the situation is accurately reflected by a verb in the passive voice. The man is a victim, and victims have things done *to* them. In addition, if the focus in description has already been on the man, the use of the passive voice allows that focus to be continued.

In other words, we use active or passive voice depending on the particular situation. Voice is choice.

> **STEP 3 (drawing and narrative)**   Write the introductory paragraph for either the drawing or the narrative. Try to use the passive voice where it is appropriate to your description.

More on Verbs (2)

Transitive and Intransitive Verbs

A discussion of the voice of verbs should also involve a discussion of the possible objects of those verbs. Transitive verbs take objects; intransitive verbs do not, and some verbs take objects sometimes and do not at other times. The verb *shine* is one that can both take an object and do without one:

OBJECT   The sun shines its light.

NO OBJECT   The sun shines.

A good dictionary will indicate, for each listing of a verb, whether it is a transitive verb (vt) and takes a direct object, an intransitive verb (*vi*) without a direct object, or both. The dictionary will also give example sentences using verbs in different ways. When in doubt it is a good idea to consult the dictionary, since as writers our problems with verbs can multiply if we are unsure whether or not they take objects.

> **STEP 4 (drawing and narrative)**   Return to your introductory paragraph. If you are unsure whether the verbs you have used are transitive or intransitive, consult a dictionary. Make any necessary corrections.

Interpretation of Meaning: Classification of Types

We have said that one main character in the drawing and the story is active while the other character is passive. These characters can be seen as *types* of people. But we can classify them as types— Tanzan and Ekido and the man and the woman—only if their behavior and attitudes seem not to belong to them alone but to characterize the behavior and attitudes of many people. We classify people abstractly as rebels, for instance (the "fish" drawing), or as escapists (the "cliff and cloud" drawing). If we choose not to employ an abstract word, we can say that they are a certain kind of person, such as the kind of person who worries a lot (the "question mark" drawing).

In any case, the first task in classifying types is to decide what we are looking for. Second, our observations should lead us to establish a specific set of characteristics. For example, we might notice that the rebel is independent, challenging, and difficult to get along with. Third, if we have truly classified a type, we will discover there is at least one other type—related to it, but different from it (often its opposite)—in existence. Opposite to the rebel is the person who accepts whatever is going on—a type that is conformist, compliant, and meek. In opposing two types, however, we must be careful that they do not overlap. If we said, for instance, that the "political type" was opposed to the "accepting type," we would soon find out that these do overlap. Political types *can* accept the status quo; therefore they belong to an entirely different pairing.

Both the "man and woman" drawing and "Muddy Road" offer opportunities for classification. The classifications we arrive at can provide the thesis sentence for this essay.

STEP 5 (narrative) Classify the types Tanzan and Ekido represent by answering the following questions about them:
a. What does Tanzan's action toward the girl tell you about his physical nature and his attitude toward other people?
b. What does Tanzan's final speech mean?
c. Does Ekido's use of the word "dangerous" say anything about his character?
d. What is the answer to Tanzan's question?

STEP 5 (drawing) By answering the following questions, classify the types of people represented in William Steig's drawing:
a. The man and woman occupy the same room, yet they each have their own weather. What does this fact disclose about them?
b. How does the difference in weather define the two of them? Is each kind of weather symbolic?
c. Does the difference in dress between the man and woman suggest what type of people they are?
d. What do their postures and gestures reveal about them?

Classifying Tanzan and Ekido or William Steig's couple gives us an opportunity to use a punctuation mark that we may not have employed earlier: the *colon*.

The Colon

A chief function of the colon (:) is to separate the name of a category or a group from the one or more items that compose it. As an example, we can briefly examine the last sentence of the previous paragraph:

> Classifying Tanzan and Ekido or William Steig's couple gives us an opportunity to use a punctuation mark that we may not have employed earlier: the <u>colon</u>.

In this sentence, the category is *a punctuation mark*. The item belonging to the category is *the colon*. The thesis sentence for an essay for this project could use the category of *types;* the items could be the types seen in the starting material.

STEP 6 (drawing and narrative)   Write a thesis sentence classifying the two types of people you observed in either the drawing or the narrative. Be sure to link your thesis sentence with the preceding introduction. Try to employ the colon as a way of connecting category and types.

In thinking about individuals and groups, we can hardly do without classification. Classification is necessary to science, the arts, and to human culture in general. Biologists have established phyla to classify the animal kingdom. Novelists allow us to see in individual behavior various types of action. And everyone distinguishes between one kind of person and another. But classification does not take us far enough. We also must be able to compare and contrast certain classifications to refine them further.

Comparison and Contrast

To *compare* two or more items is to find similarities between them. To *contrast* them is to find their differences. We can only compare or contrast items belonging to the same category. The man and woman in William Steig's drawing belong to the same category of people in general; Tanzan and Ekido are monks, a smaller category of people. But whoever or whatever it is we compare or contrast, we must have a purpose for doing so that we make clear to our readers.

Purpose

INTRODUCING THE NEW   When our readers lack information about a subject, comparing or contrasting it with a better known subject will provide further clarification for them. As in most writing projects, we would be offering our readers a service. They may not be familiar, for instance, with the idea that we are all sometimes imprisoned by doubts. But if we contrasted that state of mind with the state of mind of a fully confident person, then they might better understand our point.

MAKING A CHOICE   Often we want to tell our readers that one item is preferable to another. Comparing or contrasting the two allows us to make a convincing presentation of our choice. For example, we could contrast the realist and the escapist; in doing so, we could show that the realist, accepting responsibilities more readily, makes a better choice for a friend; or that the escapist is more fun. The choice is ours.

> **STEP 7 (drawing and narrative)**   **Decide on your purpose in writing this essay. With that purpose in mind, decide whether you will compare or contrast, or compare *and* contrast in the body of your essay. Although a contrast is more probable for either the drawing or the narrative, comparison is also possible.**

Comparisons and contrasts are made on one or more bases. Accepting responsibilities is an example of a basis on which to compare or contrast the realist and the escapist. We could show how the realist and the escapist differ (if we were contrasting) by depicting the behavior of each when faced with an identical situation. Sometimes, we can ask the same question about both items and use that as a basis. How does the man in William Steig's drawing view life? How does the woman in that same drawing view life? If each basis we choose is to be effective, then we must be careful in selecting them. Only those bases that develop major points of comparison or contrast should be used.

> **STEP 8 (drawing and narrative)**   **Choose one or more bases (depending on your instructor's directions) for a comparison/**

contrast. You should be certain that you are writing about types of people and not just Tanzan and Ekido or the man and the woman. This will help to determine your bases. Still, it might be a good idea to mention the original characters again when you write the body of your essay.

There are two major patterns for the body of a comparison/contrast essay. One pattern is to devote a separate paragraph to each basis, asking the same question of both items:

| Paragraph 1 | Basis 1 | Comparing/Contrasting A and B |
| Paragraph 2 | Basis 2 | Comparing/Contrasting A and B |

So, for instance, the first paragraph of the body might contrast the realist and the escapist on the basis of a sense of humor; the second paragraph, then, might contrast them on the basis of accepting responsibilities. The order of paragraphs follows the same general principle we have emphasized in each writing project: order of importance.

The second major pattern of organization for a comparison/contrast essay is to devote a separate paragraph to each item, using more than one basis:

| Paragraph 1 | A | Bases 1 and 2 |
| Paragraph 2 | B | Bases 1 and 2 |

In the first paragraph, either the realist's or the escapist's sense of humor and willingness to accept responsibility would be examined. Then, in the second paragraph, the same pattern would be followed for the remaining type. Again, order of importance determines the order of paragraphs.

STEP 9 (drawing and narrative)   Decide on the paragraph pattern you will use in the body of your essay. If you are writing a one-paragraph comparison/contrast, you will probably want to adopt the first pattern. Write a topic sentence for the first paragraph. Then, go ahead and write the paragraph itself.

The conclusion of a comparison/contrast essay, as with any essay, should make clear the results of extending meaning. Summary, emphasis, and significance are the three types of conclusions we discussed in Writing Project Five (pp. 104–107). For this essay, emphasis or significance would probably be most appropriate. If accepting responsibilities has been used as a basis for contrasting the realist and escapist, then we may now conclude that the realist is an essential member of any happy family. The specific qualities of the realist are now seen in a broader context.

STEP 10 (drawing and narrative) Write the concluding paragraph to your essay. Make sure that your initial purpose in writing this comparison/contrast has been achieved.

STEP 11 (drawing and narrative) Edit, revise, and rewrite your essay. To your editing checklist, add the following: the active and passive voice; transitive and intransitive verbs; and the colon as a mark of punctuation. To your revision and rewriting checklists, add classifications of types and comparison/contrast.

Interproject | *More About Verbs*

The following drawing is an alternative for Writing Project Six.

Guy Billout

EXERCISES

1. Paraphrasing prevents us from directly copying the words or ideas of another writer and presenting them as our own. This is one kind of *plagiarism*. Even a paraphrase, however, can look like plagiarism unless we identify whose work we are paraphrasing and how much of it is original with us. To draw the line between paraphrase and plagiarism, turn back to the narrative on p. 111 based on the "bridge" drawing and write a paraphrase of those two paragraphs.

2. The following sentences contain errors in verbs showing passive voice. Make corrections where necessary.

> BEFORE The man is trap by a question mark.
>
> AFTER The man is trapped by a question mark.

a. The bat was knock down.
b. The smallest fish turns around before it can be hurted.
c. The women is carry to the other side.
d. What is not knowing to the man on the bridge is whether the trio sees him or not.
e. The woman carries to the other side.

3. Change the voice of the verbs in the sentences below from active to passive voice, and vice versa. When such a change produces a version clearly not preferable to the original, put a check by it and be prepared to explain why the original is superior.

> BEFORE He is hit by the wind as he approaches the edge of the cliff.
>
> AFTER The wind buffets him as the edge of the cliff is approached.

a. His mouth is twisted to the side by his bad luck.
b. He is overshadowed by the question mark.
c. His arms are hidden from view.
d. Both his feet are planted firmly on the cloud, and yet he casts no shadow.
e. The trio floats past him.
f. Clouds gather at the end of the bridge.
g. The bat falls.
h. Cupid, it seems, has shot an arrow in the wrong direction.
i. Something bothers his head while he sits in the chair.

4. The following are verbs that you may have used in previous compositions. Look up each verb in the dictionary to discover whether it is transitive or intransitive. Then use each verb in the active voice in a sentence. If a verb both takes an object and can be used without one, write two different sentences for it. For example:

Smile

Each of the fish on the right smiles at the one in front of it.   (*vi*)

Each fish smiles the same smile.   (*vt*)

a. Rise
b. Raise
c. Escape
d. Doubt
e. Extend
f. Dominate
g. Rebel
h. Imagine
i. Transcend
j. Transfigure

5. Return to the compositions you have written previously. If you have not done so already, correct any errors in active or passive voice, and in verbs that do or do not take objects.

6. For practice in classification, what is each word in the following list a type of? What is its opposite type? Next to each type you *add*, write the characteristics that identify it.

ORIGINAL city   a type of human habitation

OPPOSITE town   fewer buildings, smaller population

a. Conformist
b. Doubt
c. Prairie
d. Pioneer
e. Love
f. Animal

7. (The following exercise is for students who, on the basis of their work to date, are considered advanced by their instructor.)

Write a composition based on one of your answers to exercise 6 above. The introduction can describe the category from which the types are taken. The thesis sentence can name both types, and the body of the essay can compare or contrast them. Referring to the original drawing will help.

REVIEW PROJECT TWO

Applying Skills; Analysis

Since Review Project One and the review composition assigned in it, there have been several more writing skills to learn and apply. On the grammatical level, most of these have involved the use of verbs. There have also been important lessons in organizing and extending meaning. The full essay has called on us to put into practice a complex of skills. Now we can pause once again to review these new skills, remembering that to review means to see again.

Either the following drawing or the bar graph may serve as the starting material for a review composition. The only specific instruction for writing this essay is to extend meaning by analysis.

Tomi Ungerer

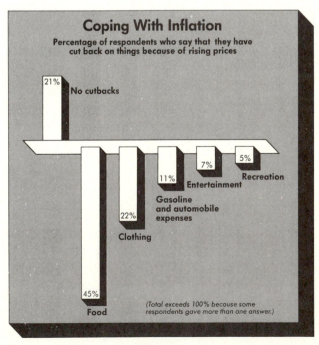

Coping With Inflation

Percentage of respondents who say that they have
cut back on things because of rising prices

21% No cutbacks

11% Gasoline
and automobile
expenses

7% Entertainment

5% Recreation

22% Clothing

45% Food

(Total exceeds 100% because some
respondents gave more than one answer.)

The New York Times and CBS

Below is a list of the skills introduced in Writing Projects Four, Five, and Six, with suggestions for their use in the present essay.

The first item on the list is *analysis*. It is included among skills for review because, without naming it, we have been analyzing each time we asked questions about the starting materials in order to interpret their meaning (see pp. 46, 48, 81, 95–96, 122). That is, we have been taking apart the drawing or story to see what it is made of. Analysis can also be used to extend meaning, however, as well as to interpret it. And so, if we are to make such a conscious use of it, we should examine the analytic method more closely.

Analysis To analyze is to separate a whole into parts so as to determine its nature or form. That whole can be anything: an institution, a group, an event, a situation, a person's character, an idea.

In an analytical essay, we start from the whole: it is the meaning or concept stated in the thesis sentence. Our aim is to understand that whole better by becoming knowledgeable not only of its parts but also of the way those parts relate to each other. We examine the whole, its parts, and their relations in the body of the essay. Once we acquire some knowledge about them, we can offer our readers a fresh view of what we started from. This fresh view we can express in the conclusion of the essay.

The first three questions on p. 122 about Tanzan, the character in "Muddy Road" (p. 117), illustrate one method of analyzing a character. Once we know something about Tanzan's friendliness, his comfortably physical nature, and his attitudes toward people in need, we will grasp essential *parts* of his character. Then, we can put these parts together to form a new idea of the *whole* of his character. We might conclude, as a result of our analysis, that Tanzan is a generous and outgoing person.

For the present essay, we can use the analytic method to extend the meaning of the drawing by Tomi Ungerer or of *The New York Times* bar graph.

Tomi Ungerer's drawing comments on one way our minds connect to what lies outside of them. The thesis sentence for an essay based on this drawing would develop a concept stating the form of this connection. This is the whole. In the body of the essay, we would analyze the concept. To do so, we could examine the typical events and situations that connect us to what lies outside of us. Each event or situation would be a part of the whole. In the conclusion, we can state a fuller idea of the connection between the individual and the outside world (emphasis), or show the larger significance of such a connection.

The bar graph gives us a big start. It is itself an analysis of inflation in the United States. The topic of that analysis is summed up by the words at the top of the graph. These words, following a description of the graph, can help us write the thesis sentence for an essay. (We should notice that the themes of both graph and drawing could be connected.)

Thesis Sentence and Conclusion   For the application of these to this review composition, see the above discussion of analysis.

Paraphrasing   The words at the top of the graph can be paraphrased. Simply to copy them (unless they were put in quotation marks) would be plagiarism, though it should be noted that it is almost impossible not to repeat precise words like *inflation* and *prices*. Probably the form of the original language is what most needs changing here, especially since that form in the graph is not a complete sentence. The terms within the graph do not require paraphrasing: as labels, they are almost as much a part of the graph as the bars themselves.

Illustration by Example, Narration, Comparison and Contrast   Analysis joins these as methods of extending meaning.

These three methods of extending meaning should be added to the revision-rewriting list compiled in Review Project One. The following items should be added to the editing list begun there.

Subject-Verb Agreement   In describing the drawing, we have to distinguish between singular *chain* and plural *links*. With regard to the graph, we should remember that labels like *clothing* and *food* are singular nouns, but that related words like *clothes* and *meals* are plural.

Verb Tenses   Since the graph measures present cutbacks, an introductory description of the graph would probably use verbs in the present tense. This means that the present perfect (*have* or *has* with the *-ed* form) will probably be useful in the body of the essay. A good dictionary gives the form of the verb used to show present tense and both forms of the past tense. This is especially helpful in using irregular verbs.

Verbs in Active or Passive Voice   In the drawing, the person is the object upon which forces of some sort are acting. The graph tells a story first of what has happened *to* people, and then of what they have done in response. The voice we use in any one sentence is a decision about what to emphasize: what is happening, or to whom it is happening.

Transitive and Intransitive Verbs   A good dictionary, we should remember, will inform us whether or not any verb can take an object.

The Colon   Describing the graph presents an opportunity to use a colon to separate the category *cutbacks* from the particular items represented in the graph. With regard to the drawing, there are so many ideas of what forces the character is chained to that the colon would probably be less useful than simply using *such as* would be. *Such as* is used when we do not expect to exhaust the category; a colon is used to develop a sense of inclusiveness.

As always, from the sentence to the paragraph to the full essay, *details*, *relationship*, and *order* should guide writing. For these to show on the page, particular attention should be paid to linking sentences by the use of connecting words.

Interproject | *Punctuation and Manuscript Style*

The following drawing is used to illustrate the discussion of punctuation. It can be reviewed whenever that would be helpful.

John Caldwell

In Review Project One (p. 69), we discussed a "code of signals" that is shared by us and our audience. Their understanding of what we write depends on our correct use of the code. An *-s* ending the word *wing*, for instance, signals a plural. Our first concern in this interproject is with the most prominent set of signals—*punctuation*.

Punctuation

Punctuation is a way of regulating the relationships of words and groups of words within sentences. It tells how final a separation between parts of a sentence is, whether those parts belong to each other or to other parts, when they all come to a halt, and more. Used properly, punctuation produces the clarity all good writing needs, as we see in the following sentence based on William Steig's drawing in Writing Project Six:

> As the sun enters, the woman's face lights up.

Without the comma after *enters, face* would appear at first to be its direct object, and therefore what the sun enters:

> As the sun enters the woman's face lights up.

With the comma, *face* is clearly the subject of *lights up*, and our readers are saved the annoyance of rereading the sentence to get its meaning.

The Period (.)

A period ends a sentence. It announces that we are now in a position to understand how all the parts of that sentence relate to each other.

The Question Mark (?)

The question mark also ends a sentence. We know to use one if the sentence begins with a word like *are, do, what,* or *why,* and if the subject follows it:

> Are the lumberjacks pushing or holding on?

The question mark can also convert a statement to a question:

> The lumberjacks are pushing?

(See Writing Project Three, p. 50, for one use of the question, and therefore of the question mark in composition.)

The Exclamation Point (!)

This punctuation gives emphasis to a statement:

> These men must reach an agreement!

The exclamation point often indicates stress or emotion and is very useful in quoted speech. But it should be used sparingly: the intensity of the writing should emerge from the language itself.

The Colon (:)

The colon divides a category from the items that comprise it:

> Each lumberjack has several options: to let go and be crushed, to let go and run, or to hold on until help comes.

The items themselves, as we see in the above example, always extend to the end of the sentence. We should note also that the terms *the following* or *as follows* usually take a colon.

The colon also announces an upcoming explanation:

> These lumberjacks obviously don't agree: one wants the world to go one way, and the other wants it to go the other way.

The explanation need not be a complete sentence. But whether it is or not, the first word after the colon is not capitalized. (See Writing Project Six, p. 123.)

The Semicolon (;)

The chief use of the semicolon is in compound sentences, where it separates two main clauses:

> The man on the left is straining himself; the man on the right is not.

Another use of the semicolon is between parts of a sentence that themselves include commas, or parts that are very long items on a list:

> Each lumberjack has several options: to let go, step back, and be crushed; to let go, turn around as fast as possible, and run; or to hold on, trust the other will too, and wait until help comes.

The above sentence, the same one that exemplifies the use of the colon, now has additional material in each item. If commas separated the items as well as the information within them, our readers might confuse these two different functions of the comma and be unclear where one item ended and the next began. (See Writing Project One, pp. 7–9.)

The Comma (,)

In a compound sentence, the comma's main function is to help the coordinating conjunction separate clauses:

> The lumberjacks may have cooperated originally, but now they are at cross-purposes.

The comma is used to separate any part of a sentence that precedes the main clause:

> Though the lumberjacks may have cooperated originally, now they are at cross-purposes. (initial subordinate clause)

> Big and bulky, each man has an equal chance to win the contest. (initial adjective)

> With their axes there on the ground at their feet, they shout at each other. (initial prepositional phrase)

> Outraged, each thinks the other is wrong. (initial past participle used as adjective)

The comma is also used to separate words in series and in lists from each other:

> The two men are digging in, pushing, and shouting.

The comma is used to separate items in dates and addresses as well as in geographical names:

> I saw a scene like this once on July 15, 1979, in Portland, Oregon.

Besides the above references for the comma, see Writing Project One, pp. 7, 8, and 12.

The Dash (—)

Dashes are mainly used to surround an inserted passage when we think its length or importance requires it to stand out from the sentence:

> These two desperate, foolish men—their memories, desires, and expectations hopelessly at odds—are locked in struggle.

Dashes are also useful to set off words at the end of a sentence. When used in this way, the dash is a stylistic alternative to the colon:

> These two men live in fear—the fear of giving in, the fear of holding on.

The Parenthesis ( )

Parentheses surround inserted passages that could be left out of the sentence without depriving it of grammatical correctness, or of information very tightly locked in to its main point:

> These lumberjacks (both of them a little crazy, no doubt) are very stupid.

The Apostrophe (')

As we have studied before, the apostrophe is used to show possession by nouns and by pronouns like *anybody, everyone, and other:*

> One lumberjack's head is bent; the other's is not.

The apostrophe is also used in contractions: two words joined to form one shorter word. Wherever a letter or letters are left out we use an apostrophe:

> They can't let go.

Can't is a contraction of *can not.* Other contractions include: *don't, isn't, wouldn't, aren't, didn't.*

Finally, the apostrophe is used to show plurals of numbers and letters of the alphabet:

> Their bodies are bent into Z's.

(See Writing Project Three, p. 54).

The Hyphen (-)

The hyphen is used to break a word at the end of a line before continuing it on the next line. We always break between syllables (a good dictionary shows these divisions):

> The tree the lumberjacks are holding extends straight up into the air.

We also use the hyphen to divide two-part words:

> Neither lumberjack is a well-meaning person.

Quotation Marks (" ")

Quotation marks surround words taken directly from another source and used in our own writing. One difficulty in using quotation marks involves the position of other punctuation marks in the sentence. It is important to remember that commas and periods, coming at the *end* of quoted material, always appear *inside* quotation marks:

> "I did most of the work," argued Bill, the lumberjack on the right. The other lumberjack replied, "That's ridiculous."

Most of the time, it is necessary to mention the source of quoted words. As shown in the above example, a comma comes between the quoted remarks and the verb (*argued*) describing the remarks. Commas are also used when a quotation is broken up in a sentence:

> "I arrived here earlier," said Bill, "and I've worked harder."

When the second part of a broken quotation is a new sentence, it begins with a capital letter, and there is a period after the first part:

> "That's ridiculous, too," said Ron. "Look at the way the trunk is cut through."

Question marks and exclamation points belong *inside* quotation marks if the quoted material is a question, *outside* if the sentence containing the quoted material is itself a question:

> "So, what's that show?" asked Bill. What could Ron say but, "Equality!"?

Semicolons and colons go *outside* of quotation marks:

> Bill said, "Big words are no answer"; however, he was puzzled by Ron's remark.

When a quotation *contains* another quotation, single quotation marks are used inside double quotation marks:

> "When I said 'Equality!' " Ron continued, "I meant that we were even."

When we refer to what someone said or wrote, but do not quote exactly, quotation marks are *not* used. This is called *indirect quotation*. Still, in indirect quotation we usually say who said what:

> Bill replied that it was all right to be even, but that Ron was always trying to get ahead.

One problem in indirect quotations involves asking questions. The word order in quoted questions is almost always inverted, with at least part of the verb coming before the subject:

> "Am I trying to get ahead now?" asked Ron, belligerently.

To quote *indirectly* such a question, we use the word order of a statement. Often the words *if* or *whether* are used in such an indirect quotation:

> Ron asked if he was trying to get ahead.

not

> Ron asked was he trying to get ahead.

Since the verb *asked* shows past time, the indirect quotation also has to be in the past. As we see, no question mark is used.

Manuscript Style

Manuscript style involves signs, marks, and arrangements of words that, like punctuation, also represent an agreement between us and our audience. Like punctuation, manuscript style is most concerned with the appearance of words on the page. The areas of manuscript style presented here include: capitalization; abbreviations and signs; underlining and the use of quotation marks; and numbers.

Capitalization

Besides beginning sentences, there are two other major uses of capitalization: proper nouns (used either as nouns or as adjectives) and titles.

Proper nouns are the names of people, countries, particular groups, races, and religions:

There are two Zen monks in the story.

Zen is capitalized because, as a noun used as an adjective to describe the monks, it names a type of religion. The word *monks* is not capitalized because it is the name only of an occupation. Russians, Indians, Christians and Jews would be capitalized. But professors, poets, and capitalists would not be. English would be; history would not.

Titles are the names of books, magazines, stories, poems, plays, articles, and so on:

"Muddy Road" focuses on just that, a muddy road.

As a title, "Muddy Road" is capitalized; as an otherwise unidentified thoroughfare, it is not. We do not capitalize *the, a, an, and, or* or prepositions in titles, unless they come at the very beginning, as we would see in a story called "Muddiness of the Road." (See p. 148 for punctuation of titles.)

Abbreviations and Signs

In formal composition, abbreviations are acceptable if they are in general use in published materials. The same holds true for signs. For instance, we see that the graph in Review Project Two is based on statistics compiled by *The New York Times* and CBS, not the *NY Times* and the Columbia Broadcasting System. One bar represents "gasoline and automobile expenses," not "gasoline & automobile expenses."

It is common practice, however, to abbreviate titles of persons, as in Dr. for Doctor or Prof. for Professor. But these abbreviations are admissible only when the titles are used with the names of the individuals themselves. We could write *Dr. Tanzan* and *Prof. Ekido*, for instance, if those gentlemen held these titles. The same holds true for the names of states used with cities and countries with states: we abbreviate the latter name only when it is attached to the former. We can abbreviate the names of organizations by using the first letter of each word in those names, particularly if the names are long. The Zen Buddhist Society for Living by the Spirit Instead of by the Letter, for instance, can become the ZBSLSIL. Sometimes, even informal groups can be abbreviated. Standard Written Expression of English Trainees can become

SWEET. And finally, with regard to signs, the ampersand (&) is popular with people in a hurry, but it is usually avoided in formal writing, as is # for number (which is often abbreviated to No.). The dollar sign ($) and the percentage sign (%) are regularly used.

Underlining and Quotation Marks

Two major functions of underlining are the following:

1. To call attention to the title of a book, a newspaper, an opera, or a movie:

   Zen Flesh, Zen Bones is the book from which this story is taken.

2. To emphasize certain words:

   Ekido thinks that above all monks should be respectable.

Quotation marks are used as manuscript style, as well as in regular punctuation, for the following purposes:

1. To surround the titles of stories or chapters taken from books, articles from newspapers, arias from operas:

   "Muddy Road" is taken from the Zen anthology, Zen Flesh, Zen Bones.

2. To isolate a word or group of words:

   "The spirit" is a difficult term to define in words, but Tanzan makes it live in action.

Indenting

When there is need to quote five or more lines of prose (and sometimes two of verse), we use a colon after the words announcing the quotation, skip a line, and indent the whole passage. This is what would be done with "Muddy Road" if it were quoted in full:

   "Muddy Road" is a short Zen story. It goes as follows:
   Tanzan and Ekido were once traveling together down a muddy road . . .

Numbers

There are various theories about how to represent numbers in writing. The convenience of our readers is probably the best guide.

For example, if it takes three or more words to spell out a number, digits are probably best: *933*. And if many numbers are used in a composition, or if some of those used have three words, we might want to use digits even for two-word numbers: *33*. Normally, two- and one-word numbers make little difficulty if they are spelled out: *twelve, sixty-three*. Whichever usage we adopt, however, *the important point is to remain consistent:* not numbers for a particular use one time and letters the next time. Dates are always written in digits: *January 13, 1979*. And sentences that begin with numbers use words, not digits: *"One thousand dollars she spent!" moaned the man sunk in the armchair.*

EXERCISES

1.   The following sentences, based on starting materials from past writing projects, have no punctuation. Use the appropriate punctuation in each sentence, and be prepared to explain the reason for each change you make. Refer to the above discussion and to the starting materials if necessary.

> BEFORE   Rube Goldbergs car a really old one doesnt look like it can move
>
> AFTER   Rube Goldberg's car, a really old one, doesn't look like it can move.

- **a.** As the bat goes down in flames Cupid just stands there wondering
- **b.** Hitting the wrong targets one mistake we make in life said Cupid
- **c.** Why was Cupids aim in life off that day he asked
- **d.** Cupid the God of Love is the one who is mistaken not the people he hits
- **e.** In the drawing Cupid is wearing his standard equipment quiver arrows bow and wings
- **f.** Hold it said the smallest fish narrowing his eyes and frowning I have other plans
- **g.** The fish who is facing the smallest fish is in a familiar position he is getting it from both sides
- **h.** The fifth fish from the left the one facing the smallest fish has an anxious moment
- **i.** In a tight corner one must do the best one can isnt that right
- **j.** One has two choices in life revolt not the easiest thing to do or accept also not the easiest thing to do

k. This stout middle aged happy woman is wearing high heeled shoes a print dress bracelets and a hair ribbon

l. The man who is no doubt her husband is obviously an unhappy creature who always takes a negative view of life

m. Its the same for all of us in this life or is it

n. A favorable wind for some people is as we see from this drawing an ill wind for others or as the saying goes one mans meat is another mans poison

o. In Tanzan Ekido sees a wrong way to do things in Ekido Tanzan sees a wrong way to look at things which is worse

p. Generosity selflessness and mutual aid are virtues who could ask for more in anyone it seems Ekido the monk in the Zen story who doesnt help the girl could

2. Continue the dialogue between Ron and Bill that breaks off on p. 146. Use both direct and indirect quotations in your writing.

3. Return to the compositions you have turned in previously and received back. If you have not done so already, correct all punctuation errors marked by your instructor. If you have been having problems with one or two forms of punctuation in particular, review their use in all your past compositions, applying to them the explanations given above.

4. Correct the errors in manuscript style in the following sentences.

a. The drawing on p. 16 of Seeing Writing shows the 12 Mythical figures of the "Zodiac."

b. 17 years ago, in nineteen sixty three, I was born under the sign of libra.

c. A Reader named Mrs. Turner did my Horoscope once.

d. When I told my prof. that my stars were in the wrong place for test-taking, he looked unhappy.

e. The Astronomy course I took did not discuss Astrology.

f. In NYC, inflation is worse than elsewhere in the US.

g. In nineteen-hundred and seventy-nine, I had to pay $1.00 for a gallon of gas and four dollars for a london broil steak.

h. The graph in "The New York Times" shows how many $ it was necessary to spend for Food, Clothing, and other items.

i. The drawing on p. 134 by Mister Tomi Ungerer shows how I feel about Inflation.

j. If that drawing was a story, its title would be Going Nowhere.

WRITING PROJECT SEVEN | # Definition; Relative Pronouns; Verbs Used as Nouns and Adjectives

Compose a full essay on the following drawing, text, or writing topic. (An alternative writing topic may be found on p. 167). Use definition to extend the statement of meaning. Employ verbs as nouns and adjectives.

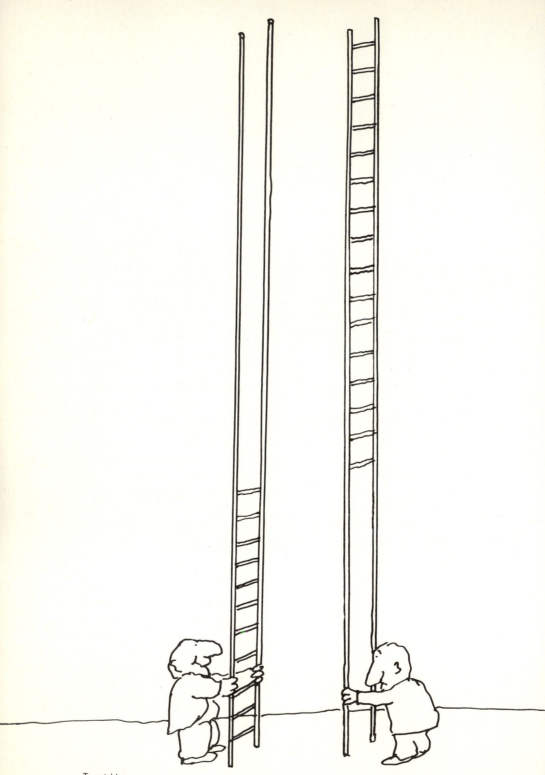

Tomi Ungerer

Text

Over the summer, when a group of about 30 widows of miners picketed at the mine to protest the slowness in recovering the bodies, the picket line was breached by miners who roared through in trucks and automobiles, shouting obscenities and insults at the widows.

Behind such actions, observers here say, is the miners' intense feeling that the mine should not be closed completely, even for a period, which would eliminate their income. Miners at the Scotia mine earn nearly $70 a day, and the incomes of some, with overtime, range to well over $20,000 a year.

Recently the miners adopted a contract negotiated by their independent company union that did not contain strong safety measures.

The head of the union resigned recently when the miners rejected a proposal to forgo their Thanksgiving gift of a ham from the company and instead use the money to establish a scholarship fund for the dead miners' children.

"They wanted the hams," the union president said.[1]

Writing Topic

Among the many types of people in this world, two of the most interesting are optimists and pessimists. Optimists and pessimists often disagree about the right way to view life: each thinks the other's position falsifies experience. Either may be right, but arguments between them will never get anywhere unless they begin by defining their terms. Here, we can prepare the ground for an effective argument by defining either optimism or pessimism. Write an essay of definition that could be useful to someone arguing for either position.

[1] From *The New York Times*, November 20, 1976. © 1976 by The New York Times Company. Reprinted by permission.

Throughout this book, we have divided composition into two related parts: description and interpretation. In an essay, the introductory paragraph describes the appearance of the starting materials, the thesis sentence interprets the meaning of those materials, and the body of the essay develops that interpretation by extending meaning in one way or another. In this chapter, we will examine one more way of extending meaning: definition.

Perhaps we can best understand definition by establishing a basic distinction between it and description.

Description reveals what something looks like—either in its physical or its intellectual appearance. As we have seen, description may be what the first part of an essay does. It may also be what a sentence used anywhere in the essay can do. Applied to the drawing in Writing Project Five, the following sentence may be descriptive:

> A person standing at the edge of a cliff has reached a dead end.

Definition calls something by a particular name so that it can be understood within certain limits. Outside of these limits is something else called by another name. The previous example sentence defines more than it describes if we ask ourselves, "What is true about a person standing at the edge of a cliff that is not true about other people?" and answer, "A person standing at the edge of a cliff has reached a dead end."

Since the same sentence can be used either to describe or to define, making our purpose in writing clear is very important. We can make this purpose felt in various ways, one of which is word choice. For instance, if we wanted to leave no doubt about our purpose to describe, we might have been more specific in the previous example and used *The* instead of *A* before *person*.

Similarly, punctuation can help make the difference between description and definition. Here are two sentences, alike except for punctuation. The first describes while the second defines:

> A person, who stands at the edge of a cliff, has reached a dead end.
>
> A person who stands at the edge of a cliff has reached a dead end.

The first sentence describes the character's physical situation with the words *who stands at the edge of a cliff*; it describes his mental situation with the words *has reached a dead end*. Though the second sentence uses the same language, in it no commas separate *who stands at the edge of a* cliff from *A person.* Here, no difference is made between physical and mental situations. The absence of commas means that this sentence defines the person instead of describing him.

To understand this difference, and to make it felt by our readers when we want it to be, we must consider a kind of pronoun—*the relative pronoun*—that can be used either for description *or* definition.

Relative Pronouns: Who, That, and Which

Who, that, and *which*—relative pronouns—introduce clauses that refer to a previous word or group of words. Relative pronouns are always the subjects of verbs and so must agree with them in number. *Who* and *that* are used to refer to persons. *Which* and *that* can refer to anything other than persons.

Often, the relative clause (which like all clauses must include a verb) occurs between the subject and verb of a sentence:

> A person, who stands on a cloud, has reached a new height.

> A person who stands on a cloud has reached a new height.

When the relative clause is surrounded by commas, we are providing further information about the subject to which it refers. But that additional information is *not* essential to identifying the subject. That is, in punctuating the first of the two previous examples we are saying that even if the words *who stands on a cloud* were omitted, our readers would still know enough to identify the subject—*A person.* Since we do not intend to distinguish one type of person from another type, the words *who stands on a cloud* are descriptive; the essential information of this sentence is: *A person has reached a new height.*

If the words *who stands on a cloud* are not set off by commas, as in the second example, the sentence takes on a new and different meaning. The information in the relative clause *who stands on a cloud* is now essential to the definition: it distinguishes *A person* from other people.

Who, that, and *which* should always fall as close as possible to what they refer to in a sentence. Because of this, they may also occur at the end of a sentence:

> He stands on a cloud that sails away from the cliff.

This sentence informs us that it is not just a cloud that he stands on, but a cloud that is sailing away. *That* identifies the cloud and is not separated by a comma from it. (Almost always, *that* is used when we do not want to use a comma.)

The following sentence uses a comma:

> He stands on a cloud, which is a new experience to him.

Here the comma signals that the *new experience* is not the cloud itself, but rather the act of standing on it. Our intention is not to define the cloud as a new experience but to describe it as that.

We can apply the distinctions between relative pronouns used to describe and relative pronouns used to define to all three of the present starting materials.

> **STEP 1 (drawing, text) Compile details for an introductory paragraph. Use *who*, *that*, and *which* wherever possible. Refer to the previous discussion and then decide whether or not you will use commas. Remember: commas describe, no commas define.**
>
> **This step is applicable to the writing topic also, but probably should wait for the upcoming discussion of it.**

Using relative pronouns can sometimes create problems in subject-verb agreement (see Writing Project Four, pp. 78–80). We should remember that the pronoun itself is singular or plural depending on the noun or pronoun to which it refers. This rule is illustrated in the following sentences:

> A person who stands at the edge of a cliff has reached a dead end.
>
> People who stand at the edge of a cliff have reached a dead end.

Though *who* is in each sentence, and is in the same position, in the first sentence it refers to singular *person* and is therefore the singular subject of *stands*; in the second sentence, *who* refers to plural *people* and is the plural subject of *stand*.

Description

We now can turn to writing the introductory paragraph for an essay based on any one of these three starting materials. Describing the physical appearance of the drawing is a familiar task and should present no new problems.

> **STEP 2 (drawing)**   After grouping and ordering the details you have collected, write a topic sentence for the introductory paragraph and then write the paragraph itself.

Describing the intellectual appearance of the other starting materials is less familiar to us and requires discussion. In this project, we are taking a somewhat new approach to the kind of starting materials the text and writing topic represent. And yet, depending on the previous work assigned, this newness may lie chiefly in the combination of skills already introduced. These combinations are what we must examine.

Text As Starting Material

To describe *The New York Times* text, it is inevitable that we will summarize, paraphrase, and possibly even quote bits in the introductory paragraph of the essay.

Summary we have discussed previously as a possible method for writing the conclusion of the essay (see Writing Project Five, p. 104). Unlike a paraphrase, which covers the whole of the original, a summary covers only the main points. It relates them to each other according to their relationships in the original and orders them according to their importance. A brief summary of "Muddy Road," for instance, might read: " 'Muddy Road' is a Zen tale of two monks, one of whose complaints about the other reveals his own mean spirit." Notice that there is nothing here about the girl, the mud puddle Tanzan carries her across (nor his action), or the lodging temple. There is only the broadest outline of the tale.

Summary is more useful than paraphrase when the original is lengthy, or when it is more important to extract and report main points than to give a picture of the whole. When there are several texts or speeches to describe, summary also becomes a useful tool. Though summary is no doubt best for the *Times* article, paraphrase was probably the best choice for the Zen tale, and it may also be useful *within* the summary here. Quotation (see Interproject, pp. 145–146) might be included in this summary as well, particularly if we want to include the union president's exact words.

STEP 2 (text)   Decide on the main points of your summary and keep only those details necessary to demonstrate them. Since a summary is often briefer than a paraphrase or a description, at this point you may need to eliminate some of the details you have collected for an introductory paragraph for an essay based on the *Times* text. Write a topic sentence for the paragraph, remembering that the characterization in it has to be broad enough to be developed by the main points in your summary, and then write the paragraph itself.

Writing Topic As Starting Material

The difference from past practice here is that the writing topic now starts from a concept: "Among the many types of people in the world, two of the most interesting are optimists and pessimists." We are at the point here that we might have reached in the thesis sentence of an essay based on William Steig's drawing in Writing Project Six. It is still necessary, however, to describe the concept. To do so, details, relationship, and order remain the principles of composition to keep in mind, just as if we were describing two linked figures in a drawing. Optimists and pessimists are the terms of the descriptive relationship here; their philosophical disagreement and the need of each type of person to define a position form the link between the terms. The words "falsifies experience" can be expanded on. We can ask such questions as *who, what, when, how,* and *why* about the terms of the relationship and the link between them (see Writing Project Four, p. 84). In the end, we must clearly establish the issue so that the thesis sentence can focus on it.

Final examinations often consist of exactly the sort of writing topic found on p. 153. These writing topics open with a sentence or two describing the issue. Then there is a direct question to answer at length, or a specific instruction to follow in writing. Often there is also a request to give reasons, cite examples, define, or compare or contrast. In working from such a topic, we may start by describing the issue, then in a thesis sentence begin to answer the main question or follow the chief direction, and following that, use the suggested method of extending meaning.

STEPS 1–2 (writing topic)   Note down details for an introductory paragraph describing the writing topic. The source of details is your own experience, knowledge, and imagination. When necessary, use the relative pronouns *who, that,* and *which,* and check for subject-verb agreement. After grouping and ordering details, write a topic sentence and then the paragraph itself.

We can now complete the first part of this essay.

Interpretation of Meaning

For either the drawing or the text, we can produce a thesis sentence in the manner familiar to us. That is, we can identify the concept that emerges from the starting materials and, in the same thesis sentence, say what those materials demonstrate about the concept.

STEP 3 (drawing)   Answer the following questions. Then write a thesis sentence based on your answers.
a. **What is the immediate difference between the situations of the two men?**
b. **How are the situations of the two men identical?**
c. **Can you put the answer to the above question in abstract terms?**

For your thesis sentence to represent in abstract form the concrete relationship between the two men, your introductory paragraph should have made their relationship clear. Check it now.

STEP 3 (text)   Answer the following questions. Then write a thesis sentence based on your answers.
a. **What was the particular reason behind the miners' action described in the first paragraph?**
b. **How does the fact that the miners signed a contract "that did not contain strong safety measures" reflect their general attitude?**
c. **What do the last two paragraphs of the story indicate about the general attitude of the miners?**
d. **Can you put that attitude in conceptual language?**

For your thesis sentence to represent in abstract form the concrete relationship between the miners and their work, your introductory paragraph should have made that relationship clear. Check it now.

The thesis sentence for an essay based on the writing topic should follow the original directions to define optimism or pessimism. This preliminary and brief definition can come straight out of a good dictionary. As we will see, the body of the essay will extend this definition.

> **STEP 3 (writing topic)**   **Write a thesis sentence that provides a preliminary definition of either optimism or pessimism. Since your thesis sentence answers a need for definition, try to express this need in your introductory paragraph.**

In moving from thesis sentence to new topic sentence, it is possible to reword the characterization of the thesis sentence in various ways. We will take up one of those ways now since it can be examined in terms of definition and description, and since it follows up on the discussion of verbs in the previous projects.

More on Verbs

Verbs Used as Nouns

Often, we find it easier to define nouns than other parts of speech. But if we wish to vary the form of words we define, and also to convey a sense of action in our sentences, we can use the present participle form of the verb as a noun. The following sentences show how the present participle can be used first as the subject of a sentence and then as an object in a sentence:

SUBJECT CARRYING the girl across the mud was no sin.

OBJECT Ekido disapproved of CARRYING the girl.

Below, we can see how using present participles as nouns can help us move from thesis sentence to the first topic sentence of the body of the essay:

THESIS SENTENCE The figure on the cliff and his counterpart on the cloud demonstrate the power of fantasy.

TOPIC SENTENCE We can see what fantasizing is, especially how it differs from imagining, if we examine its place in love.

In this topic sentence, *fantasizing* is the subject of the verb *is*, and *imagining* is the object of the preposition *from*.

> **STEP 4 (drawing, text, writing topic)**   **For possible adoption in a topic sentence, put the concept you have produced in your thesis sentence into the present participle form of the verb.**

Verbs Used as Adjectives

The present participle can also be used as an adjective to describe nouns and pronouns. This use must be distinguished from the use of present participles as nouns. The following sentences employ present participles as adjectives:

> Fantasizing about my own life, I become unhappy.
>
> The figure on the cliff, wondering what to do next, stares straight ahead.
>
> The men stood there, holding the tree and arguing.

Turning now to the body of the essay, where we produce our definition, we should remind ourselves that defining a term will require establishing the limits within which it can be recognized as what it is. The line between one concept (such as *fantasizing*) and another (*imagining*) must be made clear. To define effectively, we should be conscious of our purpose, our methods, and the results we hope to achieve.

Definition

Purpose

The purpose of all definition is to explain more clearly a particular term, concept, or idea. At times, two words can seem very similar in meaning. By defining both, we can distinguish the terms and so use them with more precision in our writing. In other instances, a particular word, like *sin*, can have as many meanings as there are individuals who use it. If we wanted the word *sin* to be clear in our writing, we would have to define it first. The clarity we gain through definition can serve more specific purposes in writing; for example, it would help us in any classification or argument. We could not conduct an argument without knowing for certain that our readers understood what we were arguing about.

Methods

One effective method of defining a concept is to examine a particular use of it in everyday life. To do so, we can produce an example—sin as viewed by Ekido, for instance—and then analyze why Ekido considers Tanzan's action sinful. This method includes two skills we have already studied: producing examples and analyzing. As always, the examples we choose to use in our definition should be appropriate to the relationships found in the starting materials.

STEP 5 (drawing, text, writing topic) Select several examples illustrating the concept expressed in your thesis sentence. Write the topic sentence for the first paragraph of the body. Cite the example you will analyze first.

STEP 6 (drawing, text, writing topic) Write the body of the essay by analyzing the one or more examples of the concept you are defining.

Results

We might want to conclude an essay on definition by first offering a one-sentence definition of the word or concept we have written about. This definition results from the analysis in the body of the essay. Even if we began with a preliminary definition (as is suggested for an essay on the writing topic), it would still make good sense to define once again.

In this final definition, we would mention the idea or concept, the category to which it belongs, and its distinguishing characteristics. These characteristics could be taken from our analysis of preceding examples. If more than one example is used, the characteristics are those the examples share in common.

The following sentence is one example of a final definition:

> Fantasy is a mental activity in which dream-like images exaggerate and improve a present reality.

Fantasy is the term we are defining; *mental activity* is the category in which we are placing it; and the rest of the sentence provides characteristics of *fantasy* that distinguish it from other similar mental activities. As in this example, most likely the final definition will be the topic sentence of the concluding paragraph.

STEP 7 (drawing, text, writing topic) After deciding on the category and distinguishing characteristics of the concept or word to be defined, compose the topic sentence of your concluding paragraph.

In the end, the significance of any definition depends on our original purpose in defining to produce clarity. Only once that clarity is achieved can the important relations of the idea or concept be pointed out. If we defined in order to extend an argument, then we can argue and expect our readers to follow our thoughts.

Whatever significance we give to our final definition, in the concluding paragraph we should mention our starting materials. They are, after all, responsible for the direction we have taken.

STEP 8 (drawing, text, writing topic)   Write the rest of the concluding paragraph, stating the significance of your final definition.

STEP 9 (drawing, text, writing topic)   Edit, revise, and rewrite your essay. To your editing checklist, add the following: who, that, and which (relative pronouns); verbs used as adjectives and nouns. To your revision and rewriting checklist, add definition as a method of extending meaning.

Interproject | *Exercises and Review*

The following article, reprinted from *The Washington Post* (October 28, 1978), is an alternative for Writing Project Seven. In the thesis sentence of an essay based on this article, we can label the woman's behavior with a term that can then be defined.

Mental Powers Provoke Accident

KITCHENER, Ontario (AP)—Incredible Mike Mandel's mental powers are too much for his own good.

The mentalist was performing at Connestoga College on Wednesday when he said using the power of suggestion he would point to a woman in the audience and she would believe she had just won the Miss Universe contest. When he pointed to the woman, she became so excited she jumped up, leaped onto his back and both tumbled to the floor.

Mandel, 25, suffered a sprained neck and will have to wear a brace and take a week off work.[1]

Other starting materials that can be used for an essay on definition are the "question mark" drawing (p. 42), the "fish" drawing (p. 76), the "daisy" drawing (p. 89), the "cliff and cloud" drawing (p. 94), the "couple" drawing (p. 109), and "Muddy Road" (p. 117).

EXERCISES

1. The following sentences, unpunctuated except for the apostrophes and the period at the end, employ relative pronouns. In some instances, there are errors in subject-verb agreement. Insert commas where needed and correct any errors in agreement. Refer to the starting materials on which the sentences are based as you work.

> BEFORE His lips which is covered are probably making muttering sounds.
>
> AFTER His lips, which are covered, are probably making muttering sounds.

---

[1] Reprinted by permission of The Associated Press.

a. Ekido who silently disapprove of Tanzan's action keeps his peace until later.

b. People who are not preoccupied with sin are more comfortable to be with.

c. The arrow which Cupid struck the bat with is not visible.

d. Men and women who want to fall in love with the right person wait for Cupid to aim straight.

e. The figure on the right who is looking out from a cliff has reached his limit.

f. Anyone in the world who are at a dead end should want a new start.

g. The lumberjack on the left who seems to be straining harder will probably win the contest.

h. Very often a project which bring people together also separates them.

i. The man's half of the cat has no more value than the woman's half which the man and woman both probably know.

j. Half of something which often is all we get is better than nothing.

2. Convert the verb in each of the sentences below into the present participle. Write one sentence using the verb as a noun and one sentence using it as an adjective. You will have to rewrite each original sentence by adding words to it.

BEFORE The chain drops out of nowhere.

AFTER (1) The chain's dropping out of nowhere tells us the man is controlled by unseen forces.

(2) Dropping out of nowhere, the chain disappears into the man's skull.

a. The arrow of love shoots into darkness.

b. The cliff represents the end before the beginning.

c. The act of divorce tears cats in two.

d. Most poor fish close their eyes to truth.

e. A Zen monk carries the world easily.

3. Each of the following sentences begins with a present participle used as an adjective. In each case, it describes the wrong subject. Find the right subject and rewrite each sentence. (The subject should immediately follow the present participle and any words that belong with it.)

BEFORE   Turning around, a mean look is on the face of the smallest fish.

AFTER   Turning around, the smallest fish has a mean look on its face.

a. Shouting at each other, the tree is what divides the lumberjacks.
b. Hitting the wrong target, the bat falls as Cupid watches in silence.
c. Pulling the cat apart, the couple's troubles have reached a high point.
d. Keeping still until nightfall, Tanzan gets to hear what Ekido has to say.
e. Looking down from the top of the cliff, the edge stops the man.

Argumentation; Logical Fallacies; Appositives and Absolutes

Compose a full essay on the following drawing, text, or writing topic. (An alternate drawing may be found on p. 183.) Use argumentation to extend the statement of meaning in the thesis sentence. Employ appositives and absolutes in writing sentences.

Guy Billout

Text

Miami, Oct. 24 (UPI)—Dade County School officials have started an experimental plan to lure truants back to classes at two schools with gifts of Frisbees, T-shirts, yo-yos and hamburgers. The program will reward teachers having the best attendance records with free gasoline, record albums and dinners.

Robert Davison, a school community liaison officer, helped develop the program to combat a problem that could cost Dade County's school system up to $3 million in state funds. The state pays school systems $824 a year for every student enrolled, but only if the student is in class when a census is taken twice a year. Last year Dade's schools had an absenteeism rate of 15 percent, or 36,000 students.[1]

Writing Topic

As it has been for some time, the divorce rate in American society is very high. The social consequences of so many marriages breaking up are as serious as the effects on the individuals involved are painful. Perhaps no one is more drastically affected than the children of parents who have decided to divorce. A question thus arises about the wisdom of divorce when there are children. In a case where husband and wife would seek a divorce if there were no other obstacle, should they stay together for the sake of the children? Write an essay arguing one position or the other: that a couple should reject divorce if they have children, or that—children or not—they should divorce if they want to.

As we see from the instructions at the end of the above writing topic, we sometimes are asked to take sides when composing an

[1] From *The New York Times*, October 24, 1977. © 1977 by The New York Times Company. Reprinted by permission.

essay. We have to choose to say *yes*, something or other is so; or *no*, it is not so. And even if we soften our position by saying that only under certain conditions is something so or not so, we still have put ourselves on one side or the other, not on both; in other words, we have to conduct an argument.

Choosing sides provides a sharp focus for writing. Sometimes we create this focus, as would be the case, for example, if we chose to write on either the drawing or the text for this project. At other times, the focus is already present in the starting materials, as we see in the present writing topic. Whichever the case, our first need when arguing is to make sure that our readers have a clear picture of the issue. We provide this clear picture through description in the introductory paragraph. This task is already familiar to us.

But, as the discussion of relative clauses in Writing Project Seven demonstrated, not only a whole section of an essay but also parts of sentences can function descriptively. One such sentence part—which can be helpful in argument by making what we are arguing about clear—is called the *appositive*.

The Appositive

An appositive is a word or a group of words containing a noun or pronoun that gives another name to the noun or pronoun next to which it stands:

> Tanzan, a Buddhist monk, is forbidden by his religion to get involved with women.

The appositive in this example is the phrase, *a Buddhist monk*. As we see, it does not start with a relative pronoun (who, that, or which), and, unlike relative clauses, it does not have a subject and a verb. In the middle of a sentence, an appositive is surrounded by commas, as the example above demonstrates. It does not name Tanzan in order to distinguish him as a monk from other Tanzans in the world who are not monks. The appositive is not an essential part of Tanzan's identity, though it does add information about him.

Like all descriptive phrases, appositives should be placed as close as possible to what they describe, as we see in the following sentences based on the drawing in Writing Project Seven:

> A happy-looking person, the character on the left sees only what is in front of him.

His position is actually the same as the person on the right, a sad-sack character who looks as if he had just been hit on the head with a hammer.

The appositive in the first sentence above precedes the comma: *a happy-looking person* describes the *character*. In the second sentence, the appositive follows the comma: *a sad-sack character* describes the *person on the right*. We should notice also in the second sentence that an appositive may help form a larger sentence part, here starting with *who looks*. We can put appositives to work right away.

STEP 1 (drawing, text, writing topic)   After collecting and ordering details, write the topic sentence and introductory paragraph for an essay based on any of the starting materials. Summary, paraphrase, and quotation are all three possible for both text and writing topic. (If you have chosen the writing topic, hold off providing reasons for your side of the argument until the body of the essay. That is where they properly belong.) In your introductory paragraph, try to use an appositive.

The appositive is also particularly useful in the actual statement of a position to be argued, as we might find later in the thesis sentence for an essay based either on the drawing or the text. The following is a model thesis sentence:

Fantasy, a dream that makes life seem better than it is, only makes happiness harder to hold on to.

The appositive in the above sentence reworks the definition of fantasy given in Writing Project Seven (p. 162). Here that definition functions descriptively as an appositive. It also reinforces the point we are contending is true.

The Interpretation of Meaning

The Thesis Sentence

In an argumentative essay, the thesis sentence states our position on a particular issue: for instance, either optimism or pessimism is the right philosophical attitude to adopt in life. But we must take care to convince our readers that our position is both reasonable and worth discussing. We are reasonable if we do not overstate our case; we qualify our position by claiming only what we believe is true, not everything that relates to our case. And our position is worth discussing if, because of general disagreement or doubt, there are two sides to the issue. We should keep the second requirement in mind as we answer the following questions to produce a thesis sentence. We should keep the first requirement in mind as we write that sentence.

STEP 2 (drawing)   Answer the following questions and, based on your answers, write a thesis sentence for your essay:

a. What is the character in the drawing doing?
b. Can the man's particular activity be seen as part of a more generalized practice?
c. What do the globe and its position symbolize?
d. How does the drawing comment on the relationship between man and globe?
e. Can you state this relationship as an argumentative issue in a thesis sentence?

STEP 2 (text)   Answer the following questions and, based on your answers, write a thesis sentence for your essay:

a. What is the school officials' main reason for combating truancy?
b. Is this a good reason?
c. Might there be another reason besides the reason reported in the *Times* article?
d. What do you imagine the effect of rewarding teachers and students in this way would be? Would it affect each group differently?
e. What kind of relationship exists between the Dade County school plan and the aims of education?
f. What conceptual term could you apply to this plan?
g. Can you state this concept as an argumentative issue in a thesis sentence?

STEP 2 (writing topic)   Answer the question about the relationship between divorce and children. In doing so, you should take a definite position on this issue. Write a thesis sentence based on your position. For this essay, the details from which your argument emerges should have been stated in your introductory paragraph. Check this now.

We can now move to the body of the essay.

Argumentation

A formal argument consists of three parts: the *position* on an issue, the *reasons* for that position, and *support* for those reasons. Taking a position on an issue has already been discussed.

Reasons

A reason answers the question *why?* about our position. "Why do we think fantasy should be avoided?" "Because . . ." we begin in response, and then go on to give our reasons. Most of us, however, know that not *all* the truth about any particular issue is on our side, that there are reasons for believing differently, even though those reasons seem weaker to us than our own. We should be fair to the other side of the argument, and one way to do so is to put in writing an acceptance of what it is right about. Though we give away something, we still remain strong by showing our readers that we can afford to be generous. This concession can be as brief as the beginning of the first body paragraph:

> It is true that fantasizing can be enjoyable, and that fun is essential to happiness. Fantasy can also backfire, however, when it conceals the true nature of people from each other.

As this example indicates, the truth we concede to the other side should have its limits, though if they are too broad, we might very well be arguing the wrong position. As we also see in this example, establishing limits can call up our own first reason for a position.

STEP 3 (drawing, text, writing topic) Write the first paragraph of the body of your essay. In it, mention the limited strength of the opposing point of view. You may want to devote a whole separate paragraph to this, or, as in the example, you may want to split your first paragraph—first referring to the opposing viewpoint, and then arguing against it.

We can find reasons for our position in various places. One place is in the definition of the concept we are supporting or opposing. If we know what characteristics distinguish the concept, we can focus on those characteristics and try to develop them.

The opposing viewpoint, too, can generate reasons for an argument. We can imagine what reasons someone arguing from that viewpoint might have, briefly state them, and then deny them with our own reasons. An argument stating that fantasy causes people to be attracted to each other might lead us to say that attraction is always based on clear-sightedness, not on fantasy.

Whatever the source of our reasons, however, it is our own knowledge and experience of the subject that allows us to use them.

STEP 4 (drawing, text, writing topic)   In the form of topic sentences, list the important reasons underlying your position in the argument. No matter how many reasons you use in your argument, make sure to lead up to the most important one.

Support

In the thesis sentence of an argumentative essay, we begin with an opinion, a very frail personal belief that our readers can take seriously only if there are good reasons to do so. We therefore must state these reasons and convince our readers of their value. But reasons are rarely self-evident: they need to be supported by evidence and explanation. The ability to support reasons, then, is the final test and justification of an argument. There are various forms of support, like the evidence of our senses and the testimony of authorities. But what we can most count on are *facts* and the *reasoning process* itself.

Facts are statements that we claim have been proved beyond dispute. We cannot use a fact as a fact in our argument until it has been proven elsewhere. Only then can it serve as hard evidence to support our reason for holding a particular position. It is a well-documented fact, for instance, that American pioneers traveled westward in covered wagons. But it is *not* a fact, because it cannot be proven, that in Steven Guarnaccia's drawing on p. 22, west is the direction in which the wagons are traveling. In arguing a position on the issue of fantasy, facts would probably not be useful in supporting any view. It just so happens that fantasy is a subject that does not lend itself well to factual documentation.

On the other hand, in the *Times* story there are quite a few facts that, if not described earlier in an essay, could be used later in it as evidence. And someone basing an essay on either the drawing or the writing topic might have personal knowledge of helpful facts.

STEP 5 (drawing, text, writing topic)   List the supporting facts for your position. The more detailed and authoritative their source, the stronger they will seem to your readers.

The *reasoning process* is the way we explain what we mean by a particular reason. No one will accept our reason without a clear demonstration of the thinking behind it; otherwise, the reason would seem to have been chosen merely to serve our own argumentative needs, not to serve the truth. A brief example of explaining the reasoning process follows:

> If we fantasize someone else as a movie star, we expect the constant beauty, intelligence, and poise that movie stars always seem to have. Most human beings, however, are not perfect. And when we begin to notice that the person we admire is sometimes dim and sometimes clumsy, we feel cheated somehow, as if we had deserved better.

We probably will use analysis, illustration by example, and comparison/contrast to explain our reasons. They can be used separately or in combination. Always, we have to guard against assuming too much, thinking that our readers share all our beliefs, even about seemingly small matters, but particularly about sensitive issues.

STEP 6 (drawing, text, writing topic)   Write the body of your essay. In the body, support your reasons with facts and explanations of your reasoning process.

Before we discuss the results of an argument, we had better make sure we have argued in the right way. The wrong way of arguing can produce untruths despite our best intentions. For instance, we might argue that in Steven Guarnaccia's drawing the wagon train is heading west because it is moving toward the left of the frame. Perhaps we have been influenced by the fact that the original covered wagons went west. And perhaps in our minds we have superimposed on the drawing a map of the United States, in which west is always left. In either case, we would have used a general rule to understand a particular instance (the drawing) without taking into consideration the evidence before us (that the drawing is not an attempt to record history; that the drawing is not a map).

Logical Fallacies

Even if Mr. Guarnaccia had told us afterwards that the wagon train *was* heading west, we would only have made a lucky guess, not used correct reasoning. We would therefore have no real way to tell if our position was true or false. There are various kinds of mistakes possible to make in reasoning. We can examine some of the more common logical fallacies:

1. *Overgeneralization* arguing, without other evidence to support our claim, that the particular instance we know of is generally true. Even if we could prove the wagon train was going west, an overgeneralization would be to claim that *all* wagon trains went west.

2. *Ambiguity* using the same term to mean two different things. If fantasy has the definition we have given it, we confuse the issue if we also use fantasy to refer to the powers of the imagination.

3. *Ad hominem* (Latin for "to the person") criticizing the person who holds a position instead of the position itself. An argument directed against sticking to the rules at all times will not succeed if we attack Ekido's personality instead.

4. *Begging the question* assuming that what needs to be proven is already proven. If we write, "The greedy miners want everything for themselves," the word *greedy* is used as if we had already proved that that is what the miners are, although we have not.

5. *After this, because of this* saying one event *caused* another simply because of the order in which they occurred. A brief story of Mark Twain's is one of the better known examples of this fallacy: "I joined the Confederacy for two weeks. Then I deserted. The Confederacy fell."

6. *Appeal to authority* saying something is true simply because an authority has said it is. If Ekido had argued that women were troublesome because a religious master had told him so, then he would be guilty of appealing to authority.

7. *Guilt by association* condemning one thing because it is associated with another that we assume everyone thinks is bad. An example of this kind of mistake is to think that the bat in the "Cupid" drawing is evil because it is a "creature of the night," and the night is (supposedly) when negative influences arise.

STEP 7 (drawing, text, writing topic) Check the reasoning in the body of your essay for the kinds of fallacies just described. If you find your argument is weakened by any such gaps in reasoning, correct them now.

A winning argument transforms an opinion into a considered judgment. By the conclusion of an argumentative essay, our readers ought to be convinced both of the truth of our view and of the correctness of our reasoning. Given this success, we are now in a strong position to do what is needed in the conclusion. We can demonstrate this strength immediately, just by the way we shape sentences, by using a new kind of phrase involving the past and present participles of the verb. This phrase, called an *absolute*, can link the topic sentence of the concluding paragraph to the body of the essay.

Absolutes

An absolute is one more descriptive phrase that qualifies a whole clause or the entire sentence. It consists of two essential parts: a noun or a pronoun and a past or present participle. The noun or pronoun acts as the subject of the participle, but the phrase cannot stand alone because participles do not show time.

The following sentences are examples of absolutes:

> All things considered, we can see the need to rid our lives of harmful fantasies.

> Fantasy seeming somewhat less necessary now, we can consider alternatives to it.

> Fantasy having become unattractive in our eyes, we can move to replace it in our lives.

In the first sentence, *things* is the subject of *considered;* in the second sentence, *fantasy* is the subject of *seeming;* and in the third sentence, *fantasy* is the subject of *having become*. As we can see, a comma separates an absolute from the main clause.

Like many absolutes, all the above phrases make a particular claim. That claim is that we have succeeded in making one point, and that this success has made it acceptable for us to make another point. The need to eliminate fantasy is clear because all possibilities have been considered. And alternatives to fantasizing can be taken up *because* its disadvantages have been exposed. The absolute expresses a claim as if it were to be taken for granted, not as if it were bragging.

STEP 8 (drawing, text, writing topic)   Write a draft of the topic sentence for your concluding paragraph. In it, see if you can use an absolute to refer to the body of your essay.

Conclusion

As we see in the above examples of the absolute, the absolute itself can *emphasize* the position we have taken in the essay. In the second example, for instance, the absolute uses the words "less necessary" to point out the negative message of our argument. The example then goes on to announce the *significance* of the original position: there are alternatives to fantasy. The remainder of the concluding paragraph could discuss imagination, for example, as a mental activity similar to fantasy and yet rooted in reality. Or we might simply recommend clear-sightedness, soberness, and facing facts.

For very long essays, the conclusion can sum up our argument by mentioning each of the major points developed in our argument. For shorter essays, the conclusion is effective if it shows the significance of our original position. Alternatives, new courses of action, the wider application of our argument—how it relates to other similar situations, why it supports or opposes other arguments—can be taken up in our conclusion. Our choice should be made according to the argument and the way we have developed it.

STEP 9 (drawing, text, writing topic) Write the final draft of your topic sentence for a concluding paragraph. Before doing so, you must decide on the significance of your position. Then write the entire concluding paragraph.

STEP 10 (drawing, text, writing topic) Edit, revise, and rewrite your essay. To your editing checklist, add appositives and absolutes (both as phrases requiring commas). To your rewriting and revision checklist, add appositives (as descriptive aids); absolutes (as connecting links in final topic sentences); and argumentation as a method of extending meaning.

Interproject | *Exercises and Review*

The following drawing is an alternative for Writing Project Eight. Schopenhauer, the person depicted by the bust in the foreground, was a nineteenth-century philosopher whose viewpoint was pessimistic. An essay based on this drawing could make a start where the writing topic for Writing Project Seven (p. 153) leaves off.

Guy Billout

Concepts from either the drawing or the text in Writing Project Seven (pp. 152–153), or from any of the starting materials listed in Interproject (p. 167) can be adopted as issues for an argumentative essay.

EXERCISES

1. Supply appositives for the following sentences. Use the number of appositives indicated within the parentheses. If necessary, look back to the original materials shown by page number. For example:

> BEFORE Tanzan and Ekido quarrel over another person. (2)
>
> AFTER Tanzan and Ekido, Buddhist monks, quarrel over another person, a young woman.

   a. During the summer, the women picketed the Scotia mine. (1) (p. 153)
   b. The average income of the miners is fairly high. (1) (p. 153)
   c. The miners decided to keep their Thanksgiving gift. (1) (p. 153)
   d. Mike Mandel got in trouble. (1) (p. 167)
   e. Mandel's injuries came when he told a woman she was a new beauty queen. (2) (p. 167)
   f. The chief event in "Muddy Road," edited by a Zen enthusiast, happens on a muddy road. (2) (p. 117)
   g. Butts has devised a strange plan. (1) (p. 2)
   h. The group on the bridge is met by a single individual. (2) (p. 36)
   i. The wagons head toward the city. (2) (p. 22)

2. Return to past compositions you have handed in and received back from your instructor. Check to see what appositives, if any,

you used in your writing. If appositives would have improved any sentences, add them now.

3.   Turn each of the following sentences into an absolute. Then add a main clause of your own making to complete the sentence. For example:

> BEFORE   The process goes from A to R.
>
> AFTER   The process having gone from A to R, the garage door opens.

a. Her fantasies turned her into Miss Universe.
b. Another person became a source of difficulty for the two monks.
c. The drivers of the covered wagons are not visible.
d. Cupid commits one mistake after another.
e. Mike Mandel got himself into trouble.
f. The miners decided to keep their hams.
g. Ekido disapproved of Tanzan's action.

4.   Return to the concluding paragraphs of your past compositions. Observe the way each concluding paragraph links up with the body of the essay and see if you can rewrite the topic sentence by using an absolute to make a new kind of connection.

WRITING PROJECT NINE | # Combining Sentences and Parallelism

Compose a full essay on the following drawing, text, or writing topic. (An alternative drawing may be found on p. 201.) Choose effective ways to form sentences and to extend meaning.

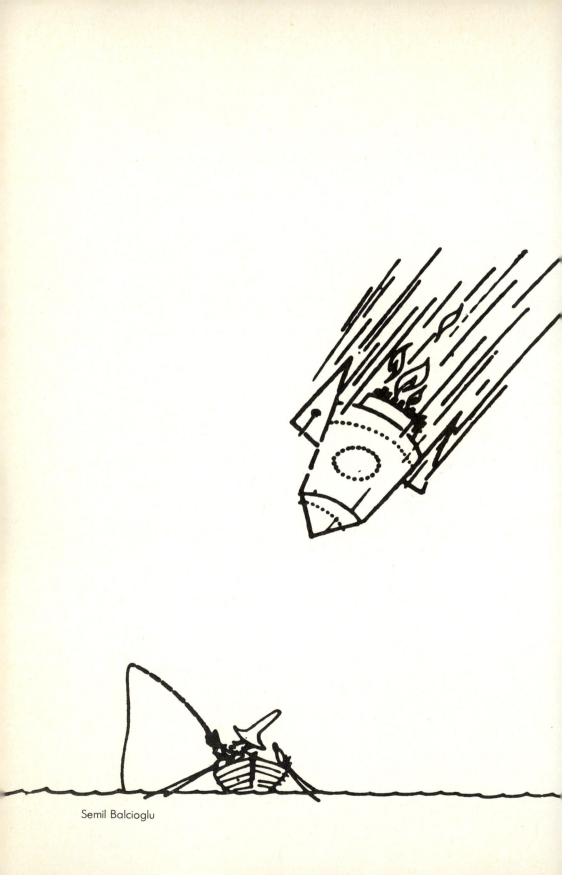

Semil Balcioglu

Text

III

I measure myself
Against a tall tree.
I find that I am much taller,
For I reach right up to the sun,
With my eye;
And I reach to the shore of the sea
With my ear.
Nevertheless, I dislike
The way the ants crawl
In and out of my shadow.

From "Six Significant Landscapes" by Wallace Stevens[1]

Writing Topic

Let us imagine two situations relating to education and work. The first one exists in Country A. There, students attend college free of charge. The government pays for their tuition, fees, books, and any other necessary expenses. Students receive a high-quality education, no matter what curriculum they are studying, and no matter what college in which they are enrolled. After graduation, they are guaranteed decent-paying, secure jobs in the field in which they have majored. But there are conditions for their free education and guaranteed jobs: the students must study what the government wants them to, live where the government thinks best, and take and keep the jobs they are given after college.

In Country B, on the other hand, college students may receive scholarships or tuition assistance; but, for the most part, they must finance their own education. Their high school preparation, as well as their own and their parents' ability to pay tuition and other costs,

[1] From *The Collected Poems of Wallace Stevens* (New York: Alfred A. Knopf, 1954). Reprinted by permission of Alfred A. Knopf, Inc.

largely determines what college they attend. Some colleges offer a good education; others do not. Following graduation, students enter the job market. Some of them fail in the competition for jobs, and jobs themselves are not guaranteed to be secure or well-paying. However, students are able to study what they want to in college. And everyone is free to choose where to live, what jobs to look for and take, when to leave a job, and whether to seek future employment or not.

Write an essay discussing these two situations. Use the method of extending meaning that you feel is best suited to the topic.

The Accomplished Writer

Every language has many forms in which it describes appearances and interprets meaning. The accomplished writer commands these forms. He or she knows what they are, how to use them, and under what circumstances it is best to use them. Part of such a writer's working knowledge is the various ways to put sentences together. Most of these ways we have studied earlier in this book. But we have not often studied sentence form as the result of choices and combinations we can be *conscious* of making.

The writer conscious of various choices may no longer need strict guidelines. For this reason, this project omits all but the most general steps in the process that formed the structure of previous projects. This project also omits questions whose use was to aid interpretation of meaning. Independence is the key word.

Choice and Combination: Sentences[1]

When we combine sentences, we make two or more sentences into one. We see such a combination in the following example based on the "Schopenhauer" drawing in the Interproject to Writing Project Eight (p. 183):

> BEFORE (1) A man sits on a small chair. (2) He looks idle. (3) His arms are crossed behind his head. (4) He gazes upward. (5) He sees the sky.
>
> AFTER Arms crossed behind his head, a man sits idly on a small chair, gazing upward at the sky.

[1] The following discussion should be studied before writing the introductory paragraph for an essay based on any of the starting materials.

As parts of the "after" sentence, "before" sentence *1* has become the main clause; *2* has been reduced to the adjective in it (now an adverb); *3* has been turned into an absolute; *4* is now a present participle used as an adjective; and *5* is a prepositional phrase. These choices have been made by adopting certain principles of combination, which are as follows:

1. A sentence can, and often should, reproduce the actual impression on the senses made by the subjects (sentences 1, 3, 4, and 5; sentence 2 would probably be an afterthought).

2. Though not actually experienced at the same time in the same place, points made by separate sentences can be joined if what counts is the relationship between them (sentences *1* and *2*). To follow these first two principles, we often must decide which sentence of several original sentences is most important.

3. All good writing is economical. (It is wasteful to keep repeating *he;* there is no need to say *sees* when the more precise word *gazes* is already there.)

In a combined sentence, there are three major positions that can be filled with parts of original sentences. Each position is related to the main clause of the new sentence, and no one position has to be filled. We can look at the following examples in order to discuss positions:

BEFORE   There are two objects near him. The objects are at his feet. One is a book. The book lies open. The other object is a glass. The glass is half-full.

AFTER   At his feet are two objects: a half-full glass and an open book.

BEFORE   There is a bust in the picture. The bust is in the foreground. It stands on the ground. The bust depicts Schopenhauer. He was a German philosopher. He was a pessimist. There is a gag in Schopenhauer's mouth. It is tied around his head.

AFTER   In the foreground, a bust of Schopenhauer, the pessimistic German philosopher, stands on the lawn with a gag stuffed in its mouth.

The positions are:

1. *In front of the main clause.* In each of the combined sentences above, a prepositional phrase is at the beginning (*At*

his feet and *In the foreground*). Often, the beginning of a sentence has the important function of linking up with the previous sentence. But the beginning does not itself contain the most important information the sentence has to convey.

2. *Between the subject and verb of the main clause.* A prepositional phrase (*of Schopenhauer*) and an appositive (*the pessimistic German philosopher*) stand between the subject and verb of the second example above. The middle is an effective place to give our readers more information about the subject of the sentence. For that reason, appositives and relative clauses often occur in the middle position.

3. *In back of the main clause.* In both example sentences more information follows the verb: in the first sentence with a compound noun (*a half-full glass and an open book*), and in the second sentence with a series of three prepositional phrases (*on the lawn with a gag stuffed in its mouth*). The end of the sentence contains what we want to emphasize. If, for instance, we had wished to call most attention to the identity of the bust, the sentence might have read: *On the lawn in the foreground, with a gag stuffed in its mouth, stands a bust of the pessimistic German philosopher, Schopenhauer.*

Mindful of the places in sentences, we now can turn to the actual choices available in combining sentences.

Compounding (see Writing Project One, pp. 6–10)

We can choose to compound sentences or parts of sentences if two or more of them repeat the same forms (adjective, clause, prepositional phrase, and so on) and relate them to each other in the same way:

> BEFORE The man has crossed his legs. Also, the man has closed his eyes.
>
> AFTER The man has crossed his legs and closed his eyes.

Because each original sentence describes the man's appearance, the contents almost ask to be combined. The combination is made possible by the identical sequence of forms in the original sentences: present perfect form of the verb (*has* + past participle), and a direct object of the verb. The forms are related by having *man* as their common subject. In the combined sentences, the second mention of the man is eliminated and the first one does double duty as the subject of both verbs. Likewise, the first *has* works for both *crossed* and *closed*.

We see the same possibility of combination in the following example:

> BEFORE   A globe falls from above. It heads for the top of his skull.
>
> AFTER   A globe falls from above and heads for the top of his skull.

The two original sentences each contain a verb taking the same subject (*globe,* and *it* referring to *globe*).

A third sentence added to the two original sentences might be *He is blind to this*. Because this sentence has a different subject (*He*), its verb cannot be compounded with the verbs of the first two sentences. But now we can write a *compound sentence*:

> A globe falls from above and heads for the top of his skull; he is blind to this.

Finding the Center

When we judge points made in separate sentences to be unequal in value, we can make one point central and think of the other one(s) as on the edge of it. The central point will be made by the main clause of the combined sentence.

One way to find the central point is to use subordinating conjunctions to form *complex sentences* (see Writing Project One, pp. 10–13). The subordinating conjunction is responsible for making one original sentence less important than another. The following examples are based on the "ladder" drawing in Writing Project Seven (p. 152):

> BEFORE   The man on the left is grinning. He sees only the bottom rungs of his ladder.
>
> AFTER   The man on the left is grinning since he sees only the bottom rungs of his ladder.

The second original sentence (now a subordinate clause) is the reason for the first (now a main clause). This particular combination makes the reason less important than the result, which is an accurate relation here. This relation would either be disguised if the two sentences were compounded or obscured if the sentences were left as they are.

Here is the origin of another complex sentence:

> BEFORE   The man on the right should raise his eyes. Then he might be happier.

> AFTER   If the man on the right raised his eyes, he might be happier.

The first original sentence is the condition for the second. The second sentence becomes the main clause. Since the verb is now in the past tense, *then* is no longer needed. The combined sentence substitutes a simple observation for the suggestion made by the first original sentence.

Relative clauses also determine the central point (see Writing Project Seven, pp. 155–156) by making one sentence refer to the other:

> BEFORE   The man on the left will finally look up. Looking up will make him stop smiling.

> AFTER   The man on the left will finally look up, which will make him stop smiling.

The relative clause (*which will make him stop smiling*) avoids repetition, closely relates the effect of looking up to the prediction of it, and recognizes the first original sentence as more important.

In the following example of three original sentences, two can be put to work for the third:

> BEFORE   Both men hold ladders. The ladders are the same height. The ladders can be joined.

> AFTER   The ladders both men hold, which are the same height, can be joined.

Since *ladders* is mentioned in all three sentences, it can be substituted for by *which* in two to make one combined sentence. Rather than follow one *which* with another, however, the first *which* can be dropped. It is now understood. But dropping *which* can be done here only because it is followed by a subject (*men*) of the verb (*hold*).

The *appositive* (see Writing Project Eight, pp. 174–175) plucks out part of a second sentence that further identifies part of a first sentence:

> BEFORE   The school rewarded former truants with the kinds of gifts children appreciate. Frisbees, T-shirts, yo-yos, and hamburgers were donated to them.

AFTER   The school rewarded former truants with the kinds of gifts children appreciate—Frisbees, T-shirts, yo-yos, and hamburgers.

The combined sentence tells us that using an entire sentence to give another name to something is not necessary, and that the information contained by both sentences should be more closely related.

Almost always, finding the center helps pare down the number of words in sentences on the edge. The *absolute* (see Writing Project Eight, p. 181) is useful as an economical measure:

BEFORE   The school district launched its program. The school district then expected a return of its original funding.

AFTER   Its program launched, the school district expected a return of its original funding.

And the reduction of words can be even greater:

BEFORE   The miners broke the widows' picket line. This happened yesterday. The miners acted violently.

AFTER   Yesterday, the miners violently broke the widows' picket line.

Yesterday and *violently* are single adverbs picked up from their original sentences. The positions they occupy in the combined sentence are not accidental. *Violently* is next to the word it describes. *Yesterday*, as a relatively unimportant mention of time, begins the sentence.

This kind of combination—of small parts of sentences on the edge—can continue:

BEFORE   Yesterday, the miners violently broke the widows' picket line. The miners were angry.

AFTER   Yesterday, the angry miners violently broke the widows' picket line.

Above, the adjective *angry* is combined.

BEFORE   Yesterday, the angry miners violently broke the widows' picket line. The miners were outraged. They were shouting.

AFTER   Yesterday, outraged and shouting, the angry miners violently broke the widows' picket line.

In the original sentences above, *outraged* is a past participle; *shouting* is a present participle. In the combined sentence, these words are used as adjectives. The sentences containing them can be combined because they have the same subject as the central sentence.

One more addition can complete the combined sentence:

> BEFORE   Yesterday, outraged and shouting, the angry miners violently broke the widows' picket line. The miners used trucks and cars.

> AFTER   Yesterday, outraged and shouting, the angry miners violently broke the widow's picket line with trucks and cars.

Trucks and cars, a compound noun, is combined as the object of the preposition *with.*

Lists and series can also be produced by combination (see Interproject, p. 143):

> BEFORE   Several animals are active in Rube Goldberg's diagram. One of them, a rabbit, runs for its hole. Two fish swim around in a glass tank and a cat is sleeping on a round table.

> AFTER   There are several animals active in Rube Goldberg's diagram: a rabbit running for its hole, two fish swimming in a glass tank, and a cat sleeping on a round table.

We should notice the use of the colon in the example. Also we should notice that *is* is eliminated from the last original sentence. The verbs *run* and *swim* change to their present participles to become adjectives (see Writing Project Seven, p. 161). Prepositional phrases are there from the beginning, as are the adjectives *several, two, glass,* and *round.*

As we see in the above combined sentences, original sentences sometimes give us the opportunity to convert one word form to another. One example of this is converting a present participle into a noun:

> BEFORE   Professor Butts wanted the garage door open as he drove up. He thought that would save him trouble. Then he would not have to get out of his car.

> AFTER   Professor Butts thought the garage door's opening as he drove up would save him the trouble of getting out of his car.

Opening is now the subject of the verb *would save; getting* is the object of the preposition *of*. In combination, the central sentence uses a subject from one original sentence and a verb from another. (There is an apostrophe showing possession in *door* because it is not the door itself but its action that will save the professor trouble in the end.)

> **STEP 1 (drawing, text, writing topic)** Write the introductory paragraph for an essay based on the starting material you have chosen. Try to combine your sentences at first writing. You should also be prepared, however, to return to individual sentences to see if further combinations would be possible.

A quick glance at the starting materials for this project will tell us that, however different the form of each is from the other, they all—drawing, poem, and writing topic—have one characteristic in common: the initial situation in each has two equal parts. The drawing has calm (boat) and violence (satellite); the poem, seeing and hearing; the writing topic, Country A and Country B. This equality in the contents of each starting material is reflected in the form of each. The drawing contains two equal images. The topic devotes one paragraph to Country A and one to Country B. In the poem, two almost identically structured sentences refer to the speaker's eyes and ears:

> *For I reach right up to the sun*
> *With my eye;*
> *And I reach to the shore of the sea*
> *With my ear.*

It is the equal form possible within sentences and between them that should concern us now that we are consciously combining sentences.

Parallelism

Within sentences, parallelism refers to repeating the same form to make related points. A sentence used earlier to demonstrate compounds is also a good example of parallel structure:

> The man has crossed his legs and closed his eyes.

This sentence gives us two equal parts: *crossed his legs* and *closed his eyes*. But, as we see in the example below, compounds are by no means the only way to create parallelism:

> He has a bald forehead, a little wisp of hair on each temple, a downturned mouth, and a large nose as round at the tip as a ball.

This sentence represents a combination of at least four other sentences describing the character in the "question mark" drawing. Each of the character's features is named by a regular noun (*forehead, wisp, mouth, nose*); before each noun is the article *a* and an adjective (*bald, little, downturned, large*).

If the structure of this example seems graceful to us, and if its parts seem closely connected, we can see that the parallelism between those parts is responsible for that grace and the connection. Or at least we can see how parallelism is responsible once we alter the way the sentence reads:

> He has a bald forehead, wisps of hair on his temples, a mouth turning down, and a nose that is large; his nose is round at the tip like a ball.

The above sentence is the result of too little calculation. Parallelism, we should remember, is a writing decision. But it is often more than a decision to be graceful and to make connections. It is also a decision to make grammatical sense and by so doing say what we want to instead of something we never intended.

Parallelism as a correct grammatical procedure can be seen in the following example:

> To have strong doubts about the future is doing work poorly now.

> To have strong doubts about the future is to do poor work in the present.

The first sentence seems to say that the *act* of having doubts is working poorly. This makes little sense. So in the second sentence, instead of *doing*, the infinitive *to do* repeats *to have*. Instead of *work poorly*, the adjective-noun combination of *strong doubts* is repeated by *poor work*. And instead of *now*, *present* is used as the object of *in* to match *future* as the object of *about*. Now there is a definite equivalence between one point and the other in the sentence. Now the sentence contains parallel structure, and now it makes sense.

And now, if we read back over the above paragraph, we should be able to see how parallelism can exist *between* sentences.

STEP 2 (drawing, text, writing topic)   Check the sentences in your first paragraph for parallel structure. Produce parallelism for any sentence that lacks it, and for any group of sentences that could use it. As you go on writing your essay, try to be conscious of using parallel forms to make related points.

STEP 3 (drawing, text, writing topic)   Interpret the meaning of the drawing, the poem, or the writing topic. Write a thesis sentence based on your interpretation.

As we remarked above, in both form and content each starting material in this project contains equal parts. The relationships between those parts can help in choosing a method of extending meaning. Comparison and contrast might work well for an essay based on any of the materials. Starting from Wallace Stevens' poem, for instance, we could contrast the situation described by the last three lines with the situation described by the first seven lines. For the writing topic, argumentation would be particularly fitting, but extending meaning through definition could be effective too. Argument would prefer the practice of one country to another; definition could attempt to understand better a concept that emerges from the relationship between both countries' practices. Narration is possible for the drawing if we could tell a story illustrating the abstract relationship between fisherman and satellite. Other methods of extending meaning are also possible for the drawing, as they are for any and all of the starting materials: we are free to choose.

STEP 4 (drawing, text, writing topic)   Choose the method of extending meaning that you find best suited to the material you have started from and most interesting to you as a writer. If, as a result of your choice, it becomes necessary to go back and revise your thesis sentence, do so now. If you need to remind yourself of a particular method, return to the project in which it was introduced. Once you have made your choice, write both the body and the conclusion of your essay.

STEP 5 (drawing, text, writing topic)   Edit, revise, and rewrite your essay. Add to your revision and rewriting checklists the conscious application of different ways to combine sentences. The following are opportunities to look for and ways to take advantage of them:

a. Different sentences that repeat the same forms and relate them to each other in the same ways (compounds).
b. Different sentences making points unequal in value (complex sentences; relative clauses; appositives; absolutes).
c. One or more original sentences adding only one or two important words to a point made in another original sentence (nouns; adverbs; prepositional phrases; adjectives; past and present participles used as adjectives).

Interproject | *Sentence Combining Exercises*

The following drawing and text are
alternatives for Writing Project Nine.

BEGLEY

James J. Begley

Text

The Cactus Plant

A young man was in line before me at the counter in Lamston's. He was holding a tiny cactus plant in one hand and a ten-dollar bill in the other. The salesclerk, a sixtyish woman with sparse, frizzy hair, was waiting for him to pay, but he didn't seem to be in any hurry. Instead, he stood looking lovingly at the cactus—a pale green spiky thing, slightly uprooted from its soil. He was saying— almost, it seemed, to *it*—that there was a sale on damaged plants, that they were selling for 79¢ apiece, and that this one looked like it was in the best shape. He thought, he said, that he could give the cactus a good home. At that point, the salesclerk interrupted him to ask for his money. He expressed surprise, apologizing for not realizing she was waiting for him to pay. He gave her the bill. She returned his change and put his cactus in a bag. As he walked off, she turned to me. Smirking, she quoted his remark about giving the cactus a good home. I didn't say anything.

—Lewis Meyers

EXERCISES

1. The following groups of sentences need combining. Use the methods discussed in this writing project. You may want to form more than one sentence for each batch of original sentences. There is no single correct version for the sentences you will produce. For each one, look back to the drawing on which the originals are based. For example:

> BEFORE There is a man on a cloud. He looks straight ahead. The cloud is fluffy.

> AFTER A man on a fluffy cloud looks straight ahead.

a. The wagons have spoked wheels. The wagons are covered wagons. They have openings in the back. (p. 22)

b. The wagon train is moving down a hill. The wagon train is following a road. The road leads to the city. The city is a modern one. The city is in the distance. It is on the horizon. (p. 22)

c. There are several oxen in the picture. They are beasts of burden. They were once used for transportation. That was in the United States. They are no longer used. They are still used in some countries. (p. 22)

d. Cupid stands there. He is in the foreground. He is the God of Love. He is nude. He has curly hair. Wings sprout from his back. Cupid has a bow and arrows. His bow and arrows are his standard equipment. (p. 35)

e. A bat falls down in the background. The bat plummets to earth. Its wings are outspread. Its beak is pointed down. (p. 35)

f. There are three people. They walk in single file. There are two men and a woman. The woman is between the two men. All of them are dressed in the clothes of royalty. They have crowns on their heads. (p. 36)

g. The single individual sees the trio. He is across from them. He is on the other side of the bridge. His hands are in his pockets. He looks like a casual type of person. (p. 36)

h. The bridge has arched supports. It grows narrow. It disappears in the distance. There are clouds. The clouds are in formation. They are on the horizon. That is where the bridge disappears. (p. 36)

i. One fish is smaller than the others. He is on the far right. He has turned around. He stares at the other fish. That fish is in front of him. The first fish is angry. The fish in front of him wants to eat him. (p. 76)

j. The smallest fish is determined. He has his own survival in mind. He wants to survive the conventional behavior of the species he belongs to. Those conventions are fatal. (p. 76)

k. Sometimes children have to behave like the smallest fish. Sometimes children have to fight back against bullies. Bullies are oppressive. (p. 76)

l. People come to a dead end in life. This happens from time to time. They resemble the man on the cliff. He cannot go any further. Then, sometimes, people dream. They dream of being in another place. They want to move to better things. (p. 94)

m. Optimists are a type of people. They look on the bright side of things. They can be compared with pessimists. Pessimists are a very different type of person. They are the opposite type. Pessimists expect the worst. (p. 116)

2. Return to your past compositions. If there is a need in them to combine sentences, do so now as practice (see pp. 190–197 above).

3. The following sentences fail to produce parallel structure. Re-write each sentence to make related points parallel. For example:

> BEFORE The man is rising, and the globe comes down.

> AFTER The man is rising; the globe is falling.

a. The path winds down the hill, and it is crossing the plain.
b. The covered wagons are standard: spoked wheels, a wooden box, canvas (it swells near the top of each wagon), and an ox to do the work.
c. While the bat falls rapidly in the background, Cupid stands still close up.
d. People who refuse to accept bullying and that are in rebellion against whatever is unjustly oppressive have a better chance to survive than those individuals just sitting back to take it.
e. Meeting people in strange costumes is to meet the unexpected.
f. One figure stands on a cliff; the other person is represented standing on top of a cloud.
g. Though reality is hard to get away from or be denied for a long time, fantasizing is possible temporarily.

4. Rewrite the sentences in your past compositions that lack parallel structure. Look for sentences in which you have related one point to another but have not repeated the form each point takes.

REVIEW PROJECT THREE	**Combining Skills and Choosing Subjects**
	Compose a full essay based on starting materials of your own choosing. (The following drawing is one possible choice.) Use the method of extending meaning best suited to your purpose. The essay to be composed here can be viewed as a final test of writing achievement.

John Caldwell

The Writer's Project

As in Writing Project Nine, for this project we will conduct our own analysis to interpret meaning; and we will decide how to extend meaning. But, in contrast to previous projects, there are no steps given here, since by now we should be capable of self-guidance. And here, we may choose our own subject matter, since self-guidance leads to freedom. Still, it might be helpful to make a few suggestions. We can look at a few of the more important choices of subject matter available to us.

Combining Concepts from Past Starting Materials

Each drawing, text, or writing topic in this book can produce a single concept or a statement about that concept. And each concept or statement (or both together) can be combined with concepts and statements derived from other starting materials. The combination can be the new basis for composing an essay. It can give us valuable experience in finding related meanings in different situations and in joining them to produce new meaning.

In Guy Billout's "Schopenhauer" drawing, for instance, the man leaning back in the chair, having laid aside the heavy book written by the pessimistic philosopher, lifts his face to the sun. The concept of happiness is one we can understand from this drawing, but it is a happiness gained by taking a particular action. A thesis sentence for this drawing might have read: "No one can be happy unless he or she chooses to be so." In William Steig's "man and woman" drawing, the woman also faces the sun. We might have previously classified her as an optimist, especially since we contrasted her with the man behind her in the armchair. And we can remember that optimism entails a positive attitude toward the future. So the concepts that result from both drawings are happiness, optimism, and choice. These are the new source of writing (we may describe these concepts themselves in the introduction, or go back to the drawings that produced them). A new statement of meaning might read: "To be optimistic about the future, one must choose to be happy in the present."

Not that this is the only possible combination of concepts from these particular drawings. Nor must the "Schopenhauer" drawing be combined only with the "man and woman" drawing. For instance, in the "couple" drawing, a book also has been put down. The "couple" drawing, and the "Schopenhauer" drawing together might allow us to combine two different ideas about reading.

Writing from New Starting Materials

The drawings and texts in this book have provided concrete materials for us to start from in order to produce abstract meaning. This meaning has always been one that was suggested or implied by the starting materials, but not stated outright by them. Such a statement has been up to the writer—to you. For this project, you may choose your own materials from which to move toward meaning. Your choice may be a drawing or a text (article, short story, poem, and so on). But it could also be a photograph or a painting or an object (a statue, a piece of furniture, or a building). Or it could be an event, an action, or a person. The possibilities are limitless so long as you are prepared to look for conceptual understanding at the end.

Writing on an Existing Body of Knowledge

Behind each writing topic for this book, such as the topic on divorce, stands a certain body of knowledge. This knowledge gives depth to any discussion you may produce in an essay. For the current project, you may choose a topic that stems from a body of knowledge you have or can obtain. One example is the effect of nuclear power plants on local communities. There is information available on this subject that you may know about or want to research. (In April 1979, the newspapers gave wide coverage to a nuclear plant accident in Pennsylvania.) Or you may have found a topic in another college course that you wish to expand on, perhaps in a paper that could also be submitted for that course. In that case, the body of knowledge may be in a textbook, or in lecture notes, or in your own mind if previously you have thought much about the subject. Alternatively, the topic could relate to knowledge you have gained on a job of some sort. For any of these, you have an opportunity to explain matters to readers who are more or less in the dark about them, and therefore to light up and make known some small part of the world.

Starting from Personal Experience

All of us, at one time or another in our lives, have had experiences that stood out in memory from other experiences. They have done so, seeming so intensely meaningful to us, because they were important to our personal development. For instance, a first summer or after-school job might have acquainted us with responsibilities we had never known. Or a particular friendship may have told us how beautiful and complicated social relationships are. There may have been a death or some other loss that affected us greatly. Or a simpler experience, like walking out into a flowery meadow bordered by pine trees on a hot summer day, might have stirred us. And did a snake slither through the grass at our feet?

These experiences, or anything like them, could have suddenly formed in us an awareness of ourselves and of our possibilities that we did not have before. For somehow, whether it is had for the first time or for the fiftieth time, a meaningful experience is one that creates in us a realization of ourselves and others. The experience lives in memory; on the page it can live in the memories of other people.

A personal experience has the best chance of living for other people if through it we can bind them to us. In writing such as we have been doing, this happens when we express a conceptual understanding of the experience. Such a concept will have its origin in an idea of what the experience means to our own life. Moving from idea to concept should be more than familiar to us, and yet it may seem more difficult in this case—starting with intuitions and ending with abstractions. We can only point out that the process of writing is the same as it has been.

Composing an essay based on personal experience, you would make the universality and totality of your realization definite in the thesis sentence. A thesis sentence for such an essay might read:

> The snake that frightened me in the July meadow told me that, for all of us, danger is sometimes hidden in what is most beautiful and what seems most safe.

You could now go on to extend this meaning by narrating or explaining later ideas and actions in your life that were formed by the earlier experience and the meaning realized from it. Or you could discuss the realization of hidden danger as it is generally present in life. The first method is a less direct sharing than the second, but both can be used to make personal experience available to all. If you extended meaning by continuing personal references, you would probably want to make a general application of meaning quite plain in the conclusion to the essay. If you extended meaning by making general references, you would probably want to make a personal application at the end.

We should also note that "experience," as the job and friendship examples show, does not have to be a single event. An experience could be ongoing, a situation that exists for you and has, perhaps, as long as you can remember. Your own involvement makes it, whatever it is, personal.

Interproject | *Word Skills*

Words

The words we use—the choices we make and the arrangements we provide—are finally responsible for our ability to bring the world and the self together on the page. This ability grows through experience and takes as many shapes as there are writers. But there is one limit on all of us who seek to be understood, and that is the nature of the language we use. Though words change in usage, and though some words go out of use altogether, these changes and disappearances are slow in occurring. Most words are firmly established. For writers who are doing the kind of writing we have been doing in this book, the firmness of the language is necessary to recognize. The discussion and exercises that follow concern some of the problems of this recognition.

Choice and Arrangement

Some words, called *homonyms,* sound alike but differ in meaning as well as in spelling. Some of the more troublesome of these are the following:

a. **apart** *separate*	The men holding ladders stand apart from each other.
a part *one piece*	Each man has a part of the solution in his own hands.
b. **brake** *to stop*	The bat is unable to brake before hitting the ground.
break *to fracture*	Cupid should break his bow in two.
c. **do** *to perform*	What could Tanzan do but carry the lady?
due *owing* (with *to*)	Was Ekido's disapproval due to his religious training?
d. **hole** *an opening*	The rabbit runs for its hole.
whole *entire*	The whole process happens quickly.

e. **know** *to comprehend*   Do the Florida schoolchildren know that the school board is bribing them?

    no *negation*   There is no reason to think so.

f. **knew** *past of* know   The miners knew what they wanted.

    new *freshly made*   They wanted a new and better standard of living.

g. **maybe** *perhaps*   Maybe the person bound by the question mark is unhappy, and maybe not.

    may be *verb showing possibility*   He may be resigned to his fate.

h. **passed** *went by*   I wonder if he ever passed them without noticing.

    past *earlier time*   That trio comes from the past.

i. **site** *place*   The best site for a city is on a river.

    sight *view*   The wagon train comes in sight of the city.

j. **their** *belonging to them*   The wagons make their way forward.

    there *word pointing to a place; word occupying position of subject in sentence*   We see the wagons here, the city there.
There are several wagons.

    they're *contraction of* they are   They're the original pioneers moving west.

k. **then** *time not present*   Cupid shot his arrow; then, the bat fell to earth.

    than *comparative term*   Shooting the wrong target is worse than hitting no target.

l. **too** *also; overly*   I too believe that meditation is too rigorous.

    to *toward; part of infinitive form of verb*   To meditate too long is to go to an extreme.

    two *the sum of one and one*   Two objects are in the drawing: man and globe.

m. **weather** *climate*   Two kinds of weather exist in one room.

    whether *if*   Some people will be pessimistic whether or not they have a good reason.

Words that are not homonyms but that are close in meaning and/or spelling can also be confusing:

a.	**accept** *agree to receive*	Most fish accept their fate.
	except *excluding*	Except for the smallest fish, the whole line faces right.
b.	**affect** *to influence*	Tanzan's action affects Ekido.
	effect *result*	Ekido feels the effect of Tanzan's action.
c.	**farther** *distance in space*	The wagons are farther away from the city than they look.
	further *distance in degree*	The wagons have further to go in time than in space.
d.	**lose** *mislay*	The captive of the question mark may lose his mind.
	loose *unrestrained*	He looks as if he will never get loose.
e.	**quite** *very* (much)	Cupid probably feels quite bad about shooting a bat.
	quiet *silent*	No doubt he will keep quiet about it.
f.	**rise** *to go up*	As the inflation graph shows, prices continue to rise.
	raise *to lift up*	I would like to raise my own standard of living.
g.	**were** *past of* to be	Perhaps the three people in the costumes were going to a costume party.
	where *reference to place*	Who knows where they came from?

We can show differences by using particular words and by adding to the ends of other words. We must take care not to confuse these usages.

a. Comparing two items, but not more than two, we add *-er* to the end of the adjective:

The fish on the far right is the smaller of the fish confronting each other.

b. When there are more than two, *-est* is used:

The fish farthest to the right is the smallest of all.

c. With the comparative word *than, -er* is used, no matter how many there are:

> The fish farthest to the right is smaller than the others.

Although usage is changing, we still say *different from,* not *different than:*

> The smallest fish is different from the others.

d. *More* or *less* can sometimes substitute for the *-er* at the end of the adjective, as can *least* or *most* for *-est.* But when *more* or *less,* or *least* or *most* is used, *-er* or *-est* is not:

> One fish is more alert than the others. It is hard to say which of the others is most unconscious.

e. Though usage is changing here too, *less* is used to take away from a singular noun, and *fewer* subtracts from a plural noun:

> Normally one would think the smaller fish had less of a chance than the others. Normally, therefore, one would think the smallest fish would take fewer risks than the others.

Nouns can sometimes be used as adjectives, as in the following sentence:

> Tanzan is a Zen Buddhist.

Zen, a noun, describes *Buddhist,* another noun. Often, however, nouns are *not* used in such a fashion:

> The double-chin man is held by a question mark.

The noun *chin* cannot be used to describe another noun. We should avoid the practice of employing a noun as an adjective unless we are absolutely certain it is generally used that way. The above example sentence could be rewritten as follows:

> The man with a double chin is held by a question mark.

Chin becomes the object of *with.* The whole prepositional phrase describes *man.*

Substitution of concrete description for abstract terms often produces imprecise phrasing:

> BEFORE   The man held by the question mark has an I-don't-care attitude.

AFTER   The man held by the question mark has an attitude of indifference.

Notice that *indifference* is a conceptual word, whereas *I don't care* is a statement the man must utter. It cannot be used as an adjective.

Speech patterns that are warm and cozy in person often waste words on the page:

BEFORE   Well, you know how sometimes people have all these questions about life.

AFTER   Sometimes people have many questions about life.

Another speech pattern wasteful in writing repeats the subject of the verb immediately after its first mention:

BEFORE   Cupid, he is the God of Love.

AFTER   Cupid is the God of Love.

The pronoun *he* refers back unnecessarily to *Cupid*, a noun that should be the sole subject of *is*.

We should try not to be redundant. Redundancy means to cover the same ground twice:

BEFORE   The man in solitude on the cliff is alone.

AFTER   The man on the cliff is alone.

In solitude says no more than *alone* does. But we would keep *in solitude* if we were going on in the same sentence to make a more elaborate point about the man:

The man in solitude on the cliff is alone because his friends have abandoned him.

The pronoun *it* cannot substitute for *there*.

BEFORE   It is three of them on the bridge.

AFTER   There are three of them on the bridge.

Note that *There* occupies the position in a sentence where the subject usually occurs but *three* is the subject.

In giving a reason, the word *because* is not used to identify that reason:

BEFORE   The reason is because it does not want to be eaten.

AFTER   The reason is that it does not want to be eaten.

EXERCISES

1. Choose the correct word or words within parentheses for each of the following sentences:

    a. The smallest fish is not really (apart, a part) of the line.
    b. Like the woman convinced she was Miss Universe, people can (loose, lose) control.
    c. The (effects, affects) of inflation are very severe.
    d. A bat is (different from, different than) what Cupid expected to hit.
    e. The descending satellite (maybe, may be) going to hit the fisherman.
    f. We don't know (whether, weather) or not the man on the bridge is surprised by what he sees.
    g. The man lost in meditation (raises, rises) toward the globe.
    h. Good attendance will bring the school (quiet, quite) a lot of money.
    i. The woman in "Muddy Road" is the (least activist, less active, least active) of the three characters.
    j. (It, There) appears to be no life in the city.
    k. The man on the cliff has (sort, sought) a way out for a long time.
    l. Tanzan and Ekido could have gone (passed, past) the woman.
    m. "This is (to, too) much!" I exclaimed when I read the inflation graph.
    n. The miners, as (their, there) union president (new, knew), (were, where) thinking of themselves first.

2. The following sentences contain mistaken usages. Correct them by rewriting the sentences.

    a. The buildings, they have many windows.
    b. It's kind of like when you see someone in the street or something wearing a bow-tie.
    c. The sun will benefit our welfare better than reading Schopenhauer.
    d. The reason for this elaborate scheme is because Professor Butts is too lazy to get out of the car.
    e. The on cloud nine man has escaped his problems.
    f. The figure on the cloud is the more taller of the two.
    g. It is a man sitting and meditating.
    h. The man on the left holding the ladder has a ladder with no top rungs.

   i. Which ladder man has less rungs on his ladder then the other has?

   j. The miners, all of them were just thinking selfishly of themselves, if you know what I mean.

3. Rewrite the following paragraphs, correcting errors in usage:

   a. Wallace Stevens, he wrote a poem that sort of says people are limited and have restrictions on them. They can use there ears to hear sounds much further away; they can see sites in the distance; but it is nothing they can do to escape themselves. The reason for thinking this in the poem is because the ants move in and out of the speaker's shadow. The speaker cannot loose that shadow; it clings too his feet, and the ants that have past through it have a bad effect on his sense of dignity. Do to them, also, he knows he will die, that all humans will, and that the technology advance age we live in cannot save us.

   b. The cactus plant man probably was just thinking weather he could successfully rise the plant he was buying. That's the reason, you see, he failed to notice the woman waiting to except his money. His mind was farther away from the transaction then hers was. The woman, she was businesslike than he was. But she was to impatient. The way I see it, I think it was no reason for her to laugh at him. She treated him in a sort of isn't he stupid way. It's easy to loose our feelings for others, to stand a part from them and forget were there minds are at the moment. The woman in this story maybe an object lesson for us: we should be more kinder to others.

4. Return to past compositions and correct any mistakes in word choice or word arrangement that you may have made and not corrected up until now.

INDEX

223

A   0
B   1
C   2
D   3
E   4
F   5
G   6
H   7
I   8
J